Before Beaumont Hamel

The Royal Newfoundland Regiment

1775 - 1815

B.D. Fardy

Before Beaumont Hamel
The Royal Newfoundland Regiment
1775 - 1815

B.D. Fardy

Creative Publishers
St. John's, Newfoundland
1995

The publisher acknowledges the financial contribution of the *Department of Tourism and Culture, Government of Newfoundland and Labrador*, which has helped make this publication possible.

Appreciation is expressed to *The Canada Council* for publication assistance.

∝ Printed on acid-free paper

Published by
CREATIVE BOOK PUBLISHING
a division of 10366 Newfoundland Limited
a Robinson-Blackmore Printing & Publishing associated company
P.O. Box 8660, St. John's, Newfoundland A1B 3T7

Printed in Canada by:
ROBINSON-BLACKMORE PRINTING & PUBLISHING

Canadian Cataloguing in Publication Data

Fardy, Pernard D., 1949–

    Before Beaumont Hamel

    Includes bibliographical references
    ISBN 1-895387-58-2

1. Great Britain.   Army.   Royal Newfoundland Regiment
2. Canada — History — War of 1812 — Regimental histories —
Newfoundland.   3. United States — History — Revolution, 1775-1783 —
British forces.   I. Title

UA652.R826F37   1995   356'.189'09'7 18   C95-950285-8

In memory of the "Blue Puttees"
and the men of all the Newfoundland Regiments
who served, bravely and faithfully,
for country, freedom and Peace . . .

and for
Jack, who appreciates it . . .

and for Walter A. Tobin,
last of the "Blue Puttees"

WALTER TOBIN
(1898 – 1995)
Veteran Royal Newfoundland Regiment 1556
Last survivor of the Battle of Beaumont-Hamel, July 1, 1916

Table of Contents

Preface

HIS BRIEF CHRONOLOGY of the "Royal" Newfoundland Regiment is meant to cover only a brief forty year period of the regiment's by now more than two hundred year history. The title "Royal Newfoundland Regiment" may at first suggest to some that what follows is misleading. There is no intent to mislead, as the Newfoundland Regiments, although fully raised in, and composed of Newfoundlanders over the more than two centuries of its on again off again existence, have been called by many titles. Some of the regiments have had the honour to have been distinguished with the prefix "Royal" appended to their title, others have not, and still more had been attached to other, long established British regiments which already bore the prefix "Royal."

Whether they served as members of the "Royal" Newfoundland Regiment, the Newfoundland Volunteer Corps of Foot, His Majesty's Newfoundland Regiment of Fencible Infantry, or were attached to such time honoured corps as the King's Orange Rangers, the Royal Americans or the Royal Highland Emigrant Regiment, all the men of Newfoundland who served their King and country bravely and faithfully deserved the honour of having the prefix "Royal" appended to their regimental titles.

B.D. Fardy
October, 1995
St. John's, Newfoundland

Chapter One

Ordeal by Fire: The Siege of Quebec

HE "BLUE PUTTEES" are Newfoundland's most famous and venerated fighting force in the long history of our island as a colony, country and Canadian
province. Yet the Royal Newfoundland Regiment, so venerated for its part in the "Great War," was not the first one in
our history and hasn't been our last. It survives today and has
existed since the American War of Independence. For over
200 years the Royal Newfoundland Regiment has existed; to
fight, be disbanded, be absorbed by other regiments, be
re-organized, and fight again as an independent force which
first and foremost belonged to Newfoundland.

It had its glorious moments such as at Beaumont Hamel,
but it also had its moments of ignominy such as the St. John's
mutiny of 1800. Newfoundland Regiments fought to save
Quebec from invading Americans during the American
Revolution, and helped keep Toronto for the British during
the War of 1812. They were the first of her colonists to rally to
her aid at the outbreak of the "war to end all wars"—World
War I.

In the summer of 1775, the British learned that most of
their "New England" colonies in America had determined to
revolt and secede from the mother country by force of arms.
They also learned that the rebellious colonies intended to

"convince" the less enthusiastic colonies, or "provinces" to the north of them, by the same means. The New England colonies had been making overtures of annexation to the colonies and "provinces" of Newfoundland, Nova Scotia, New Brunswick and Quebec, for some years. The rebels seemed certain that their most likely ally would be "Canada," or Quebec, which had only fifteen years earlier been conquered by the British on the Plains of Abraham and wrested from the power of France.

The French-Canadian "habitants," the New Englanders thought, would be only too glad to be liberated from their oppressive conquerors, and thousands of them would join the Rebel colonies in their revolt. Quebec was also isolated from the coast, well inland with a border contiguous with the American hinterland, and also, lightly defended along its hundreds of miles of border on the shores of the St. Lawrence River and the Great Lakes.

When the word reached Governor Guy Carleton of Quebec that the Americans planned an invasion of the country, the governor immediately began to plan its defence. He had only about 1,000 regular troops under his command and most of them were spread out up the St. Lawrence River to defend Montreal and other outposts against an American attack on the St. Lawrence down the Richelieu River from Lake Champlain.[1]

Carleton left Quebec City under a small garrison and went with the other men he could spare to the front at Montreal where the main American attack was to come. Before he left the Canadian capital, he left instructions for his officers to conduct an intensive recruitment campaign throughout the northeastern colonies of Canada. There was little response from Nova Scotia, New Brunswick and Prince Edward Island, all of whom had precious few men they could spare to help defend Quebec at the risk of leaving their own colonies open to attack. Little help was forthcoming from England either; the home country had its hands full in Europe with France and Spain.

Carleton's commandant in his absence was Lt.Col. Allan MacLean of the 42nd Regiment of Foot, who upon receiving no response from the closest colonies, decided to recruit in the "far off" island colony of Newfoundland. MacLean's reasons for recruiting in Newfoundland are not entirely clear, but his success there was. MacLean ordered two of his Captains, Colin Campbell and Alex MacDonald to rush to Newfoundland and attempt to raise a regiment of fighting men.

MacLean had authority from Commander-in-Chief of British forces in North America, General Gage, who wrote him from Boston on June 12, 1775 that he was "...empowered by beat of drum or otherwise, to enlist for His Majesty's Service in any of His provinces in North America such Highland, or other loyal subjects as you may be able to procure, to be formed into a corps. The whole corps to be clothed — armed — and accoutered in like manner with His Majesty's Royal Highland Regiment and to be called the Royal Highland Emigrants."[2]

After their dismal failure in the Maritime provinces, Captains Campbell and MacDonald found themselves a bonanza in Newfoundland. But it was not mostly Scots Highlanders that they found willing to join them. Their efforts of recruitment were carried out for the most part on the Avalon peninsula and in St. John's, where they found most of their volunteers to be Irish "youngsters"—young men who had come to Newfoundland to work in the fishery, but who were young, brave, and foolish enough to try their hand at war. Some of them, Campbell recognized as of other value than soldiers. There was a surfeit of skilled artisans and carpenters in St. John's, and the Captain saw his chance to hire these skilled men to prepare the badly crumbling defences of the citadel city of Quebec. In late October he sent 100 of them to the Gulf of St. Lawrence and up the St. Lawrence River where their arrival was hailed as a godsend by the Royal Engineer in charge of the fortification of the city.[3]

Captain James Thompson of the Royal Engineers wrote: "While employed at this section of the work, a company of artificers arrived from Halifax and another company from Newfoundland joined me soon afterwards — windows were barricaded, leaving only loopholes for Musketry." The Newfoundland "artificers," however, were expected to do double duty. Thompson reported; "...after completing the works of defence, I with all my artificers were called upon to do duty as soldiers and ordered to join Major John Nairne's party as a Corps de Reserve...I had to mount picket with my artificers who were armed from nine at night until daybreak and again resumed our labours at the fortifications."[4]

On November 12, 1775 Capt. Campbell arrived in Quebec City with forty of his Newfoundland recruits, and the following day, a British frigate of twenty-six guns followed him with ninety more of the Irish-Newfoundland colonists. He reported to MacLean that fifty more recruits from Newfoundland were waiting in Halifax for transport up the St. Lawrence, and that by Christmas he hoped to have 500 more ready to march up the St. Lawrence.

However, both the weather and the Americans were moving too fast for the British. Winter closed in early on the Gulf of St. Lawrence blocking it with ice and preventing Campbell's fifty Newfoundlanders from leaving Halifax; and the Americans closed in early on Montreal almost preventing Carleton from leaving for Quebec City.

At Montreal, Carleton found himself facing a force that outnumbered his scattered forces by two to one. After sharp and decisive engagements at the Upper St. Lawrence outposts, he found himself having to retreat to Montreal after suffering 200 casualties among his preciously few forces. There, he decided that further resistance would mean annihilation, as Montreal was indefensible, and he retreated with a handful of his men to Quebec City where he hoped he could make a stand and save the country.[5]

Back in Quebec City, the Governor was relieved to find that the tiny garrison of about 130 men he had left to defend the place was now more than doubled, thanks to the timely arrival of the recently recruited Newfoundlanders in the Royal Highland Emigrant Regiment. Now, along with his 960 regulars, and about 1,400 Canadian militia, (many of whom had chosen to stay only because MacLean had threatened to kick them outside the city walls if they did not take up arms), Carleton found he had a fighting force of 1800 men.

Although he knew the strength of the American force that would be pursuing him down the St. Lawrence River from Montreal, he did not know how many were in the second force that had by now cut off the city from all outside contact. Carleton had served with Wolfe on this very site, the Plains of Abraham, in 1759 where he now found himself on the defensive and he was not about to repeat the mistakes of the French commander Montcalm who had lost the city, and the country, to the British only sixteen years earlier.

Outside the walls of the fortress city the second prong of the American two tined attack had dug in. It was led by the later to be infamous traitor to the American cause, Colonel Benedict Arnold. He arrived on the south shore of the St. Lawrence River opposite Quebec City on November 8, and waited for word from his American sympathizers within the

Col. Benedict Arnold left Maine with an army of 1100 to attack the citadel city of Quebec in 1775. By the time he reached there, almost half of his men had fallen victim to the winter weather, fatigue, and sickness.

citadel. He had hoped that the city would be lightly defended since he had received word from his counterpart at Montreal that Governor Carleton had gone to the aid of Montreal. What he did not know was that just a few days after his arrival on the south shore of the river, the city had been reinforced by the Royal Highland Emigrants from Newfoundland and that almost two weeks after his arrival the Governor himself had slipped back into the city under his nose.[6]

Colonel Arnold settled in to await the expected victorious force from Montreal. On December 2nd, Brig. General Richard Montgomery arrived at Quebec City after having defeated the British on the Upper St. Lawrence and capturing Montreal. He and his forces arrived, ludicrously in better shape than Arnold's. Although Montgomery had engaged the enemy, his casualties were less than Arnold's, who had begun with 1,100 men and now sat on the banks of the St. Lawrence River with only 650, of whom 100 were too weak or sick to fight.[7]

By now, Col. Arnold had the citadel city cut off and surrounded for over two weeks and knew it could expect no relief since the ice had choked off the Gulf of St. Lawrence. His commander, Montgomery, decided to continue the siege that Arnold had begun and attempt to starve out the defenders.

The siege of Quebec continued for another month, the American commanders only making small forays against its walls to keep their men from becoming disgruntled and bored. The Americans had a force of 1,100 men, and knew that the reinforced British had as many as 1,800 inside the city walls. But Montgomery was determined to have a successful ending to his campaign. He knew also that his position was tenuous. Deep winter would soon be setting in and his supply lines would be cut off. A long siege might see his army become the victims, exposed to the savage elements of winter while the British waited them out in the shelter of the fort. Montgomery, like Carleton, had also served on the Plains of Abraham at the Battle of Quebec in 1759, and fully realized that his old comrade in arms inside the city was not about to repeat Montcalm's mistakes.

By the end of December, Montgomery and Arnold had decided to move. They would wait for bad weather and darkness and penetrate the walled city through what was called the "lower" town of Quebec City at the slopes leading up to the fortress. On the night of December 31st, the Americans got their bad weather in the form of a furious snowstorm. Staging a diversion on the heights of the plains in front of the city, Montgomery and Arnold led their men along the shoreline paths and backroads into the "lower" town.

Governor Carleton had anticipated such moves and had spent the two months of siege to prepare for them. He had every road, trail or pathway leading up the slopes from the "lower" town blocked by heavy barricades and manned by detachments of soldiers and cannons. Alert sentries of the Royal Highland Regiment which manned the barricades spotted the infiltrating Americans and spread the alarm. Montgomery who was leading one of the attacking forces suddenly came upon one of the barricades in the blinding blizzard. His men hesitated a moment, unable to see much through the swirling snow. Montgomery, to spur them on, drew his sword and shouted; "Come on brave boys! Quebec is ours!"

As the Americans pressed forward four cannons behind the barricade exploded with a belch of grapeshot that cut a wide swath in the advancing rebels' line. The gallant Montgomery was killed instantly as were two of his officers and ten of his men. The surprised Americans scrambled to retreat dragging their wounded companions through the snow with them.

On the other side of the "lower" town, Col. Arnold and his men ran into the same stiff resistance from the Highlanders and Newfoundlanders. They beat back several attacks by the Americans with musket fire and cannon shot, wounding Arnold himself with a musket shot through his thigh. The American commander's wound was so severe he had to be carried from the field.

Arnold's second in command, Major Daniel Morgan, succeeded in breaching the barricades with a small band of his frontier riflemen as the cannons were being reloaded and scattered into the houses of the "lower" town. He hoped to hold the town until Montgomery's men penetrated the defenses and joined him to assault the slopes leading to the fort. He did not know that Montgomery had been killed and his men were in retreat.

While Morgan waited, the Highlanders and Newfoundlanders did not. Led by Captain McDougall, 120 of them rushed down into the "lower" town to flank the houses that Morgan and his men had occupied. Within minutes, squads of the Highlanders and Newfoundlanders were rushing among the buildings, bursting through doors and clearing the houses room by room in hand to hand combat that saw British bayonets against American tomahawks and longknives.

Morgan and a handful of his men held out for the night but by morning were isolated in one of the houses. About ten o'clock on New Year's morning of 1776 he finally surrendered. The remnants of Montgomery's contingent was in retreat and most of Arnold's men had either been killed or captured. Quebec City had been saved for the British, largely due to the alertness, valour and ferocity of the Royal Highlanders and the Newfoundland Regiment.

But the Americans had not given up on their plan to capture Quebec in spite of their first defeat. The siege of Quebec began, overseen by Col. Arnold who was recuperating from his wound. He sent to Montreal for reinforcements and called for General George Washington to send him further support.

Outside the walls of Quebec City, Colonel Benedict Arnold kept expecting a breakout by Carleton but after a month of besieging the citadel city and huddling in the snow and freezing temperatures of the Canadian winter, short of rations and suffering from smallpox, the American soldiers were weakened physically and disheartened morally. It became a matter of time as to whose reinforcements would arrive first. Arnold received his first, but as he was still suffering from his wound, he was evacuated to Montreal. His successor however, proved to be indecisive and he made no move against the besieged British.

Inside the walls of Quebec City, Carleton's British regulars and Canadian militia were not faring much better than their enemy without. Food was getting scarce and hard to come by, having to be smuggled into the city where it was sold to the military defenders at exorbitant prices by mercenary blackmarketers. The winter proved to be one of the worst in years, and "snow in some places drifted twenty feet high." Many mornings, officers and enlisted men alike were ordered out to parade with "shovels and snowshoes" to clear the snow clogged roads and ensure access to the defensive batteries.

The bitter winter weather took a heavy toll on the soldiers. The morning after one particularly cold night, the officer of the guard on making his rounds of the sentry posts walked past one of the sentries who did not challenge him. The officer halted the sentry and angrily demanded why he had not been ordered to halt. "God bless your honour," the man replied, "I am glad you are come, for I am blind. The officer found the soldier's face to be frostbitten white and his eyes frozen shut. He was too weak to walk to the guardhouse so the officer carried him there to be thawed."[8]

Carleton had the church bells of the city silenced and gave orders that "The Great Bell of the Cathedral is not to ring, but in case of alarm; when it does ring every man is to assemble at the Grand Parade." Although the Americans made no outright attack on the walled city, they kept up an harassing sniping fire on the guardposts. The sniping took its toll. Almost daily the duty officers reported casualties: "A sergeant of the Emigrants killed by accident." "A soldier of the Emigrants wounded mortally in the head." "A man of Colonel MacLean's regiment of Captain Malcolm Fraser's company killed on the two gun battery."[9]

Under the harsh siege conditions, discipline became difficult to maintain and as nerves grew raw and morale sank to near defeatism, the few officers of the Royal Highland Emigrants found their authority contested. One of Col. MacLean's junior officers openly contested his authority and quarrelled with him for which the junior officer was forthwith courtmartialed and drummed out of the service. Many of the city's civilians, if not outwardly sympathetic with the Americans, showed a discouraging apathy towards their predicament and only served to compound the military's dilemma.

By mid March, after two and one half months of the brutal seige, orders were given to the soldiers that, "Every man (is to sleep) in his clothes, his arms and accoutrements to lay by his side." The order was almost lip service to most of the Newfoundlanders who by now had not changed their clothes, or in some cases, even taken them off for four months. On March 14th, Col. MacLean issued orders that "every man in the garrison is to sit up all night and be together in bodies."[10]

The British had learned through their spies, or otherwise, that the Americans may be planning an attack on the city on St. Patrick's Day, when they expected most of the garrison, since they were Irish-Newfoundlanders, to be drunk in celebration. Col. MacLean had his regiment assembled and "asked" them if they would postpone their "celebration" until May, when it was expected they would receive relief and reinforcements up the St. Lawrence River. It was a measure of MacLean's leadership and a measure of his men's loyalty that, as one officer recorded in his journal on St. Patrick's Day, 1776, "Greatly to the credit of the Irish, not a man was seen the least in liquor."

When the American spies reported that St. Patrick's Day had been cancelled in Quebec City, they abandoned any plans they had of attacking the fortress. The siege of Quebec continued for another seven weeks, then with the approach of spring came British reinforcements. On May 6th, the sails of H.M.S. *Surprise* appeared in view of the citadel, and behind it the *Isis* and *Martin*, filled to the gunwales with 8,000 British regulars and German mercenary troops.[11] After landing his relief supplies and troops, Gen. Carleton readied his plan to break the siege of Quebec.

By May 16th, he was ready. He now had a force that outnumbered the enemy by eight to one, and after their miserable and squalid winter they probably did not even know it. But before he broke the siege of Quebec City, the Governor had one small piece of business to conclude. That morning he issued a General Order to the men of the Royal Highland Emigrant Regiment: "Ordered by the approbation of the General (Carleton), that the Sons of St. Patrick do meet Col. MacLean on the parade tomorrow at eleven o'clock in the forenoon to drink grog."[12]

With their promised, belated, Paddy's Day celebration under their belt, the Newfoundlanders of the Royal Highland Emigrants led the march out of the besieged citadel of Quebec onto the Plains of Abraham.

PROFILE; SIR GUY CARLETON; DEFENDER OF CANADA.

National archives of canada C-2833

Sir Guy Carleton, Governor of Quebec

Governor of Canada and Commander in Chief of British forces, Carleton successfully defended the country against the American invasion and seige of Quebec in 1775-1776.

Guy Carleton who, perhaps unwittingly became the defender of Canada was neither English-Canadian, French-Canadian, or even Canadian at all. He was an Irishman, born in 1724 the son of a poor country gentleman at Strathane, County Tyrone. At an early age he joined the British Army and made the military his lifelong career. He was a young officer with General Wolfe at the Plains of Abraham in 1759 where he was wounded in the head outside the citadel walls of Quebec City. In 1761 he was with the British invasion fleet off the west coast of France where he was wounded once again. The following year he was in the Caribbean where he was wounded a third time at the Battle of Havana.[13]

By 1766 he was in Canada and that year the Governor of Quebec was recalled to England. Carleton was given the rank of General and appointed to replace him. He was now forty-two years old, a tall, straight-standing, slightly balding man and still a bachelor. He was described by men who served under him as a "grave man, one of the most distant, reserved men in the world. He has a rigid strictness in his manner which is very unpleasant and which he observed even to his most particular friends and acquaintances."[14]

With his new appointment, Carleton found that he had inherited the old problems of his predecessor. He was charged with implementing the terms of the treaty of 1763 that had brought an end to the war between France and England which saw all of French-Canada turned over to the English. Over the next several years however, Governor Carleton found himself supporting the same views that had gotten his predecessor replaced. Carleton felt that the French-Canadian population might join in with the grumbling American colonies to the south in revolution if their traditional rights were not safeguarded.

By 1770, he felt so strongly that the Americans were near rebellion and were wooing the French-Canadians to join them, that he left for England to lay his proposals for ensuring the allegiance of the Canadians to the British crown before the Houses of Parliament. His stay in England became a prolonged one as he lobbied the political powers. During this time he courted and married the comely, twenty year old daughter of a blue-blooded English family. Lady Maria Howard had two children by the time the Governor was ready to return to Canada.[15]

When he arrived back in Quebec in 1774, Carleton not only had a new family with him but also a new deal for the French-Canadians. He had succeeded in getting the British government to legislate the Quebec Act. The Act guaranteed the French-Canadians the right to their own language, customs, and religion, and an oath of allegiance that contained no reference to religious persuasion.

The Quebec Act cooled the resentment of the French-Canadians towards British rule as well as to the overtures of the American malcontents. Carleton had arrived back in Quebec with the document just in time. The next year the American colonies began their War of Revolution and their first target was the seat of British government in Canada at Quebec City. By the fall of 1775, the American "rebels" were on the march towards Quebec.

Carleton found he had very little with which to defend the country; in all about 1,000 regular troops, including about 150 men of the Newfoundland Regiment just recently arrived from the island colony. The British outposts strung along the upper St. Lawrence River as far as Montreal had very few men to defend them so Carleton dispersed his small force among them as evenly as he could. What he was counting on was raising an army of as many as 18,000 men in a French-Canadian militia to help aid in the defence of Canada.[16]

When the Americans finally moved on the St. Lawrence in the fall of 1775, the militia Carleton had hoped for did not materialize. The British posts along the Upper St. Lawrence fell quickly to the invading Americans and then Montreal too, where Carleton was when it was attacked. However, the Governor and a handful of his men succeeded in evading the Americans and escaped downriver to Quebec City.

The Americans attacked the old city on the stormy new year's eve night of 1775. Carleton's defences had been well planned, and the two pronged attack by the colonial rebels led by General Richard Montgomery and Colonel Benedict Arnold was stopped by Carleton's small, but determined forces. Montgomery was killed and Arnold wounded, and the Americans settled in to lay a long winter siege to the walled city.

With the spring, Carleton received reinforcements and broke the siege of Quebec City, routing the Americans and pursuing them up the St. Lawrence River where he captured his outposts and regained Montreal, the Americans having deserted it in the face of his large advancing force. Carleton chased the rebels all the way back to their wilderness fortress at Ticonderoga, deep in Ohio county but as winter was coming on did not intend to repeat the mistake of the Americans by laying siege to a fort that could hold out throughout the winter, only to be reinforced in the spring to route a weakened and disheartened army. Accordingly, Carleton withdrew his forces to Quebec City and awaited further developments.

The Governor was criticized by the home government for his failure to press his attack on the Americans at Ticonderoga, and in 1776 he was replaced as commander-in-chief of the British forces in Canada, although he retained his post as Governor of the colony. He remained at odds with his superiors for the next year until finally in the fall of 1777 he resigned his post as Governor of Canada. He waited out the winter until his replacement arrived in the spring of the following year, when he departed for England.[17]

By 1782, the war in America had been going badly for the British and they re-called their commander-in-chief, Sir Henry Clinton. To replace him, they once again called on Guy Carleton, who this time was sent to negotiate peace with the Americans. He landed in New York in May and arranged for the evacuation of British troops there as well as loyalist settlers who were sure to be displaced once the peace treaty had been signed in Paris. The British troops he had no problem removing, the loyalist settlers he could only offer the safety of Nova Scotia or New Brunswick.[18]

Following the War of American Independence, Carleton once again returned to England, and as well it seemed, so did his favour with the British authorities. Four years later in 1786 he was returned to Canada with the new title of Governor-General of Canada. His appointment would see him as the supreme authority over all the Lt. Governors of all the

Canadian "provinces." He was a popular choice with the Loyalists of Canada for they viewed him as the man who had saved their country at Quebec in 1775 and saved many of their lives in New York in 1783.

Carleton continued in the office of Governor-General of Canada for ten years, until his retirement from public life in 1796 at the age of seventy-two. He returned to England to live out his retirement where he was later knighted for dedication and service in the "colonies" of North America. Sir Guy Carleton died in England at the age of 84 years in 1808.[19]

Sir Guy Carleton served his "adopted" country as soldier, statesman, politician and Governor for almost forty years from the Plains of Abraham to Government House at Quebec City. He probably did more to defend and preserve Canada both on the battlefield and in the political arena, than any other man of his time in North America. Although not born a Canadian, he "became" a Canadian, and has earned a place as one of the country's most respected "adopted" sons.

Endnotes:

1. Raddall, Thomas H.; *The Path of Destiny*, p.33.
2. Saunders, Dr. Robert; "When Newfoundland Helped To Save Canada." *Newfoundland Quarterly*, Vol. 49, No. 3, 1949. p.19.
3. Ibid. p. 39. Lt. Col. MacLean had complained to his superiors during the summer of 1775 that he was "in no state to stand a siege," and that "except for a few of my own regiment and the seamen, I cannot get a man to repair the works."
4. Ibid.
5. Ibid. p. 20 Carleton escaped Montreal in a voyageurs' cargo canoe "skipped" by a man named Joseph Bouchette, known on the St. Lawrence as the "Wild Pigeon." Bouchette's knowledge of, and skill on the river, allowed Carleton to reach Quebec City, eluding the American force which by now had arrived at Quebec city and effectively had it blockaded.
6. Every, Dale Van; *A Company of Heroes: The American Frontier 1775-1783*, p. 85. The thirteen New England colonies not only wanted to secede from Britain but also wanted Canada to go along with them. They had enticed Newfoundland with whom they had had long and good trading relations, but also wanted to embrace Quebec, or "Lower Canada" into their familial arms. They thought that Quebec, which was French-Canadian, would prefer to embrace them rather than the British to whom they had lost their independence only a short fifteen years earlier on the Plains of Abraham in Quebec.
7. Raddall; op. cit., p. 24. Col. Arnold and his 1,100 men set out on their trek through the trackless wilderness of western Maine and were caught by an early winter. They suffered severe hardship from the weather, exertion, and hunger. One of his men recorded in a journal that "they had a Newfoundland dog; but food became so scarce that it had to be killed and made into a broth ... He was a large dog and very fat."
8. Saunders, op. cit., p.36.
9. Ibid.
10. Ibid.
11. Lanctot, Dr. Gustave; "When Newfoundland Saved Canada." *Newfoundland Quarterly*, Vol. 49, No. 3, 1949, p. 9.
12. Saunders; op. cit., p. 42.
13. Dupuy and Dupuy; op. cit., p. 252.
14. Dyer and Viljoen; op. cit., p. 27.
15. Raddall; op. cit., p. 9.
16. Dyer and Viljoen; op. cit., p. 42.
17. Raddall; op. cit., p. 66.
18. See endnote number 5.
19. Dupuy and Dupuy, op. cit., p. 252.

Chapter Two

Marching as to War:
The American Revolution

O N "ST. PATRICK'S DAY" morning of May 16, 1776, Governor Guy Carleton and his regular troops and Canadian militia broke the siege of Quebec City. Formed up in traditional battle formation, dressed in their best battle uniforms, and led by the beat of drums, the British marched out of their besieged fortress after six months onto the Plains of Abraham to take the fight to the enemy.

From the two gates of the citadel city, Carleton led out at the head of his 800 regular troops who had steadfastly weathered the long, winter siege. They deployed and formed up on the Plains of Abraham, and although a small army, as one observer put it; "it was an impressive one, stretching as it did quite across the historic ground from bluff to bluff and glistening with steel."[1]

The Newfoundlanders of the Royal Highland Emigrant Regiment, led by their "eager and restless" commander Col. MacLean, occupied the place of honour on the field, the advance "right" guard, filed out under their blue, red-bordered standard, possibly the only time that a Newfoundland Regiment carried its own colours onto the field of battle. The centre of the field was taken by the Maritime "artificers," again, many of whom were men from Newfoundland, but now instead of hefting hammers and saws, they wielded swords and muskets.[2]

The Americans, unaware that the British had been so heavily reinforced, at first attempted a resistance, Their advance outposts fired a few volleys of musketry but when

Governor Carleton reviews his troops before marching out of Quebec City to break the seige of the Americans in 1776.

Carleton's cannon came into play from the heights of the walls of the city, the Americans quickly broke and retreated. They had spent a more wretched winter than the British; all of them were fatigued and hungry, and most of their ranks had come down with smallpox.

After their feeble resistance, the Americans "fled most precipitately as soon as our field pieces began to play on their guard houses; they left cannon, muskets, ammunition, and even clothes; we found the road strewed with muskets as we pursued them; clothes, bread, pork, all lay in heaps on the highway."[3]

Newfoundland Museum

Soldier of the Royal Highland Emigrant Regiment: Raised mainly in Newfoundland, the regiment fought at the siege of Quebec in 1775 and throughout the American War of Independence 1776-1783.

The men of the Royal Highland Emigrant Regiment were first into the abandoned American camp, quickly seizing and manning the American batteries in case of a counter-attack. But the Americans were not regrouping — they were retreating. As the British settled into the abandoned American camp, a British officer gloatingly recorded; "...upon the disappearance of the Americans, MacLean's Regiment, the Royal Emigrants, sat down to eat the dinner of the American General which they found ready upon his table."[4]

Carleton was in no hurry

to follow. He knew the weakened American force would stop at Three Rivers where they would be augmented by the rebel force there. Now having enough of a force with him, Carleton took three days to reach Three Rivers, but once there his attack was quick and decisive. The weakened American force put up little resistance before they retreated to Montreal. At Three Rivers, Carleton recaptured the foundries and forges that had been supplying his American besiegers with their cannon and musket balls.

The Governor was anxious to press the retreat of the rebels and try to capture Montreal, but he knew his men were too weak and weary from the long winter siege to take on a foot-slogging forced march up the St. Lawrence River. His force was also considerably smaller than the American one he expected to meet at Montreal. He wisely opted to await the arrival of the fresh troops from Quebec that were following upriver in troop transports.

While Carleton waited, the Americans did not. They mounted a counter-attack on Three Rivers on a dark night in late May. The American scouts and guides proved to be not too reliable and the colonials blundered into a stout defense erected by Carleton. Again the Highlanders and Newfoundlanders met the Americans with withering volleys of musket fire. A small group of the British troops flanked the attackers and within minutes the Americans were routed and retreating in disarray.

The British took 200 prisoners on the spot including their commander General Thompson. Carleton chose not to pursue the retreating Americans and risk exposing his flanks to possible attack, but instead to hang on at Three Rivers and wait for his reinforcements to catch up to him.

By June, Carleton's garrison at Three Rivers had been reinforced by 6,000 British troops and 4,000 German Hessians (mercenaries hired by the British Government). The British commander prepared for his advance up the St. Lawrence River and his final task, the recapture of Montreal. Before he was ready to march he received the pleasant news that the Americans had retreated from Montreal on June 15th, after learning the strength of the British forces that would be marching on them. All the American troops along the upper St. Lawrence had withdrawn to Fort Ticonderoga, a bastion of defence deep within their own territory. The huge, strong fort was located at the head of Lake Champlain which emptied into the St. Lawrence via the Richelieu and as such was the access of the Americans to the Canadian border. Although deep within rebel territory, Carleton knew that Fort Ticonderoga was the launching point for the invasion of Canada and could be used to launch a second offensive.

Carleton marched his force up the Richelieu River to the bottom of Lake Champlain and there began to build a "navy" for an assault on the massive and strong fortress of Ticonderoga.

The Americans were also building a "navy" which was to be commanded, once again by Carleton's nemesis Col. Benedict Arnold. On October 5, 1776 the two navies, comprised of a ramshackle collection of armed schooners, galleys, gondolas and whaleboats mounted with a single cannon in their bows, sailed towards each other from opposite ends of the lake.

Col. Arnold, although less experienced as a "captain" than Carleton, proved to be the better strategist — at least at first. He surprised the British "fleet" from behind a headland in a cove but it was not long before the superior experience and firepower of the British gunboats were winning the day. By nightfall most of the American fleet had been sunk or disabled but under cover of darkness Arnold himself and a few of his boats slipped past the British line and made it to the safety of the fort.

The following day Carleton gained the shore and surveyed the huge fort's defenses. He could only have found the situation to be ironic. He could see at a moment what Arnold inside the fort must also have seen. It was the siege of Quebec all over again, only this time it was Carleton who was on the outside looking in. He knew the strength of the fortress was about his own, 10,000 men. He also knew that a siege at this time would be disastrous. He was more than 200 miles into enemy territory and his supply lines would be that long to Montreal and Quebec beyond. His troops were not outfitted or provisioned for a winter campaign and the Americans enjoyed one advantage he did not have at the siege of Quebec City.

The colonials had an open supply route to the south, through friendly country with good roads. Those roads could also bring American reinforcements which could cut off Carleton's supply lines and starve him out in the bitter northern winter. Carleton could only have grinned wryly at the prospect, while within the fort Arnold must have smiled widely.

Some of Carleton's officers were in favour of an all out frontal assault on the fort before the November snows set in. The Governor understood their eagerness, for they had been victorious in every encounter with the invading Americans since the siege of Quebec City. Their wily commander casually pointed out to them that Colonel Abercrombie of General Wolfe's command had thought the same thing in 1758 and that the bones of his men were still mouldering under the debris around the skirts of the huge fortress.[5]

On November 2nd, Carleton made up his mind. He decided that he would rather be the besieged than the besieger. He struck his camp and marched back down the Richelieu to the St. Lawrence and Montreal. There, he fortified the town, leaving several thousand troops behind to defend it. He felt confident the Americans would not try another winter attack knowing that the gateway to the Canadian border was so strongly defended with thousands of reserves available from Three Rivers and Quebec City.

His fortifications secure, Carleton took his Highlanders and Newfoundlanders back downriver to Quebec City where he arrived during Christmas of 1776 to a hero's welcome. He and his Highland Emigrant and Newfoundland Regiments had executed a flawless campaign with the invaders whom they succeeded in repelling back across the border. Canada had been saved for the British and the Loyalists.

The contribution of the Newfoundland "Regiment" to the siege of Quebec in 1775 was not overlooked by their commander-in-chief. Governor Carleton wrote the home government praising their courage and performance. "They have gone through the service all the winter with a steadiness and a resolution which could hardly have been expected from raw, undisciplined troops, and for which they cannot be too much commended...the artificers from...Newfoundland shewed great zeal and patience under very severe duty and uncommon vigilance."[6]

The commanding officer of the Newfoundlanders, Colonel Allan MacLean, expressed pridefully; "No troops could have behaved better than my young men!"[7] Other military observers saw the presence of the Newfoundlanders and the Royal Highland Emigrant Regiment as crucial to the preservation of Canada. One officer was convinced that; "Had it not been for the Highland Emigrants, Quebec would have fallen, and had Quebec fallen, British prestige west of the Atlantic would have ceased to exist."[8] Another commented; "From the oldest British Colony these volunteers (Newfoundlanders) went rushing to the help of the newest sister province. Few in numbers, but strong in patriotism, they brought to Quebec a moral support and priceless reinforcement in a war in which forces were small and every soldier precious. And they came when most desperately needed, when a feather could have turned the scales and meant the loss of Canada...In the military annals of Newfoundland there is no more inspiring page of patriotism, endurance and bravery..."[9]

Following Carleton's decisive victory over the invading Americans, the Newfoundland contingent of the Royal Highland Emigrants was returned to Montreal for a long overdue and well deserved tour of "easy" duty. The Regiment was headquartered in Canada's second "city" throughout the winter of 1776-1777 to garrison the town against any further attack. In June of 1777, Col. MacLean was promoted to the rank of Brig. General and installed as commander-in-chief of all forces at Montreal, which included his by now famous Regiment of "young men." That year, MacLean petitioned the king to have his newly formed, and battle proved regiment installed on the regular army list. His appeal went unheeded but not unnoticed. He had Governor Carleton on his side and the Secretary of War in London looked favourably on his request. He wrote Carleton that; "Col. MacLean and his officers have shewn such zeal for the service and are spoken of so advantageously by you that I trust they will receive some mark of his Majesty's favour."[10]

The next year, MacLean journeyed to England to make a personal appeal to the King on behalf of his regiment. He proved successful, and when he returned to Quebec his "young" Highland Emigrant Regiment had become His Majesty's 84th Regiment of Foot. The King's new Regiment continued to serve in the American War of Revolution, guarding what was later to become the international boundary between the United States and Canada.

While the men of the first "Newfoundland Regiment" did duty in Canada, the Americans heated up their struggle for independence. The British found more and more need for "loyal" recruits from its colonies as more and more young men from the thirteen American colonies took up the torch of "freedom." Recruiting efforts went badly in Nova Scotia and New Brunswick where forces were energetically at work to win those colonists over to the American side. Once again, the British looked to their oldest and most isolated colony of Newfoundland, where the seeds of sedition had not yet been sprinkled on sympathetic soil.

By October of 1778, the "loyalist" regiments in the American colonies were hard pressed to survive. Their ranks suffered heavy casualties and they were plagued by desertions as more and more young men joined the American "cause." As a result, some of the regiments were ordered to retreat to the more "stable" colony of Nova Scotia where it was hoped they could recruit "loyal" young men. One of them was raised in Orange County, New York, by Col. John Bayard and given the title of the King's Orange Rangers. By 1778 the regiment was down to 317 rank and file and it was decided that it should try to raise 700 men to fill its complement of 1,000.

That summer, two Captains of the K.O.R. (King's Orange Rangers) were sent to Newfoundland on recruiting duty. The following summer it was reported to Halifax that the K.O.R. Captains Brice and Rotton had "met with great success in recruiting so great that they are embarrassed to find ships to transport men from hence. (St. John's). The several recruiting parties in this and the neighbouring harbours have recruited seven hundred men — all fine stout fellows."[11]

The Regiment of the King's Orange Rangers was now more a Newfoundland Regiment than a "loyal" American one. Some of the K.O.R. Newfoundlanders were detailed to duty in Nova Scotia following the aborted "rebellion" there, but most were attached to regular British forces and sent to battle in the Carolinas in the southern "rebel" colonies.

In 1779, the British pushed their offensive in the Revolutionary war from the south of the American colonies, attacking north through Georgia and the Carolinas. The

Newfoundland Museum

"Drumming Up" recruits on the streets of St. John's in 1800. the army had little trouble getting men to join up in the fall of the year when the fishery closed down for the season. But each spring many deserted to return to the fishery which paid better wages.

Newfoundlanders of the K.O.R. were under command of Lt. Col. Thomas Brown and that year they invaded and captured Fort Augusta, Georgia and soon had the whole territory secured. Col. Brown and a few companies of the Orange Rangers were detailed to garrison Fort Augusta and were greatly outnumbered the following summer when the Americans counter-attacked.

Realizing the town was not defensible, Brown withdrew his men to a position in the hills nearby and settled in to await reinforcements. The Americans took Augusta then moved on Brown's men and demanded their surrender. With Brown's refusal, the Americans attacked but could not dislodge the Rangers. After taking heavy casualties, which included Brown himself who was shot through both thighs, the American commander again called on Brown to surrender.

Brown replied that it was "his determination to defend himself to the last extremity."[12] Despite repeated attacks, the Rangers held out for four days until reinforcements arrived and routed the attackers. Over the next couple of years of the war, companies of the Rangers were detached to serve under Cornwallis, Rowdon and Tarleton, and did duty all over the Carolinas and saw much action. In 1782, companies of the 84th Royal Highland Emigrant Regiment joined them from Quebec and the Newfoundlanders of both regiments fought side by side once again in a foreign land.[13] The "Newfoundland" Regiment saw some of the most savage battles of the Carolinas campaigns and fought in some dozen actions from Augusta, Georgia to Charleston, South Carolina. By 1782, the ranks of the King's Orange Rangers were so badly depleted that it was recalled to Nova Scotia.

There, its officers once again began a recruitment campaign and once again they headed off to Newfoundland. The reputation they were earning as solid, fighting men had

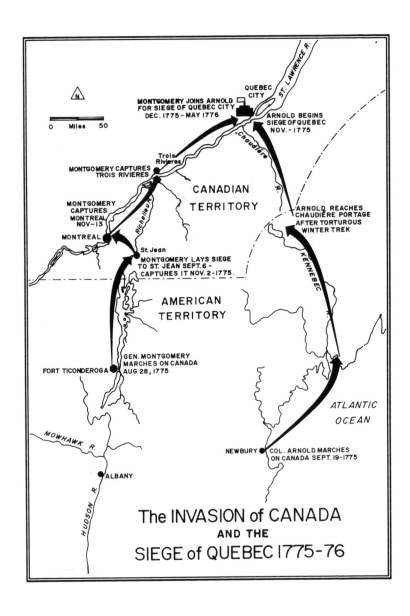

The INVASION of CANADA
AND THE
SIEGE of QUEBEC 1775-76

placed them in great demand and won them great respect. But before the Rangers' ranks could be replaced the American Revolutionary War came to an end and the King's Orange Rangers were disbanded in 1783. Most of its veterans settled in Nova Scotia on land grants offered them for their service to King and country, but for hundreds of them the only land they could claim were lonely gravesites — in a now truly "foreign" land.[14]

PROFILE: THE NOVA SCOTIA REBELLION

While most of Capt. Campbell's Newfoundland Regiment was seeing extensive action in Quebec and New York against the American rebels, the small company of fifty who had been stationed in Nova Scotia were feeling a little useless serving on standby in a "loyal" British colony. Their feelings of uselessness were soon to change.

Ever since the rumblings of dissent had begun to roll in the thirteen colonies to the south, architects of the American Revolution had felt and proposed that the colony of Nova Scotia should become the fourteenth of the thirteen colonies of America to proclaim their independence from Britain. Proponents of the theory claimed there was great sympathy for the American cause in the colony and it would take very little effort to capture the peninsula and convert all Nova Scotians to the cause of freedom, justice and equality.

A plan to invade and win Nova Scotian colonists to the American cause was proposed to General George Washington at the same time that Col. Benedict Arnold proposed his for the invasion of Quebec. Washington balked at any plan that included sea manoeuvres since the Americans had nothing even closely resembling a navy, and the Royal Navy's prowess and skill was known worldwide. Instead, the American Commander-in-Chief opted for the plan of Arnold and put the plan to take Nova Scotia on hold.

After Carleton's rout and defeat of Arnold's attempted invasion, the Nova Scotia plan now looked appealing. There already existed a secessionist movement in Nova Scotia, headed by several prominent citizens of the colony. They saw their opportunity to carry out their plan in the summer of 1776 when the large force of British troops stationed in Halifax withdrew to New York as the news of Carleton's defeat of Arnold reached them.

The rebel Nova Scotians proposed to the Americans that the colony could now easily be taken as it was garrisoned only by 300 British regulars at Halifax — most of whom were ill — a weak garrison of Boston loyalists at Fort Cumberland guarding the isthmus to the Nova Scotia peninsula, and a small company of Newfoundlanders serving with the Royal Highland Emigrants stationed at Windsor in the Bay of Fundy.

The Nova Scotia insurgents were promised help from Boston and they pressed on with their plans, raising as their advance guard a company of enthusiastic frontiersmen from the settlement of Machias, Maine. The Nova Scotian rebels and their Maine allies marched on Fort Cumberland in the fall of 1776. On route they stopped at farms along the St. John River in New Brunswick recruiting sympathizers. In late October they arrived at the town of Cumberland and announced to the people of the town and the farms nearby that they were an advance party of a large American Army sent to liberate Nova Scotia. Many of the local people joined them and the "army of liberation" marched on Fort Cumberland.

Colonel Gorham, in charge of the ragtag group of Bostonian "loyalists" in the fort, did not take the threat of the apparent rabble of American backwoodsmen and local farmers very seriously. He was prepared to sit behind the walls of his well-built fort and wait them out.

In Halifax, there was grave concern among the "Bluenose" loyalists and the Governor tried to rally the settlers of the Annapolis Valley and Minas Basin to arms to march in support of Fort Cumberland. To his amazement, he could not raise a single company of men. Most were indifferent to the situation but what the Governor found even more alarming was that many of the settlers, even the merchants of Halifax, were in sympathy with the American rebels.

The commander of the Halifax garrison, General Massey, recognized the seriousness of the situation and decided to act on his own. Most of his troops were sick or disabled and the remainder of them would be needed to maintain order in the town. He had two companies of Royal Marines from two warships in the harbour landed and sent them overland to join up with the small company of Newfoundlanders at Windsor in the Bay of Fundy.

From there the Marines and Newfoundlanders set sail up the Bay of Fundy in two small ships towards the isthmus. The ships ran into foul weather and became separated, the one with the Newfoundlanders going astray in the thick fog. The Marines succeeded in landing below the fort and during the night made their way across the fog-bound marshes and into the fort.

With the rebels secure in the knowledge that the fort was cut off from support, Gorham laid out a plan to strike first. Late at night the Royal Marines and Gorham's troops stole out of the fort and encircled the rebel camp. At first light they attacked, catching the "liberators" by surprise. In less than an hour the "army of liberation" was on the run. The British troops followed closely, burning the farmhouses of the "sympathizers" they encountered along the way.

Half the retreating rebels did not stop until they reached the safety of Machias in Maine. The other half, led by a man named John Allen, halted at the mouth of the St. John River in New Brunswick. Throughout the winter of 1776-77, Allen spent his time recruiting a new band of rebels from among the villagers up along the river. He also courted the support of the Malecite and Micmac Indians of the area.

In Boston, the Americans still did not recognize their opportunity to capture Nova Scotia, but in Halifax General Massey took the threat seriously. He spent the winter of

1776-77 recruiting more troops for a campaign against the rebel base on the St. John River. He found his new troops among the Scots of Cape Breton, Prince Edward Island, and again, Newfoundland. By early summer of 1777 he had assembled a force of 600 Royal Marines and 400 Royal Highland Emigrants which included Campbell's Newfoundland Regiment.

Massey had to keep a large part of his force at Halifax for fear that the Americans would make a daring strike at the colonial capital. He sent a detachment of marines and Highlanders and ordered them to join Gorham's troops in the Bay of Fundy from where they would strike at the St. John River. In June, the attack force, loaded aboard three warships, sailed for New Brunswick. Gorham's troops surprised the rebels and after a brief resistance they broke and fled upriver. The Newfoundlanders and marines followed close behind in small boats and canoes, encountering small groups of the rebels who stood to make a stand. All of them were overrun by the pursuing British and the farms along the river left in flames.

Allen retreated far upriver to join his Indian allies. The Malecite and Micmacs, learning of the strong force they would encounter, realized they would be on the losing side and deserted the Americans and their Nova Scotia allies. The British fell on the remnants of the "Army of Liberation" and destroyed it. Allen made his escape back to Machias but Massey was unrelenting in his pursuit.

In late August he sent a squadron of Royal Navy ships against the American town and when they sailed away the Maine port was ablaze, its defenders killed or scattered. With its head severed, the snake that was to be the "Nova Scotian Rebellion" died.[15]

Endnotes:

1. Saunders; op. cit., p. 46.
2. Lanctot, Dr. Gustave; "When Newfoundland Saved Canada." *Newfoundland Quarterly*, Vol. 49, No. 3, 1949. p.9.
3. Saunders; op. cit.
4. Ibid.
5. Raddall; op. cit. Col. Abercrombie had an army of 15,000 when he attacked Fort Ticonderoga which was defeated by Montcalm in 1758. In one day he lost almost 2,000 men killed, wounded or missing.
6. Lanctot; op. cit., p. 13.
7. Ibid.
8. Saunders; op. cit., p. 40.
9. Lanctot; op. cit., p. 10-11.
10. Saunders; op. cit., p. 35.
11. Ibid.
12. Ibid.
13. Dupey, Ernest and Trevor N. Dupey; *An Outline of the American Revolution*, p. 212.
14. Saunders; op. cit., p. 11.
15. Raddall; op. cit., p. 80-84.

Chapter Three

The Regiment Comes of Age

FTER THE FAILURE OF THE NOVA SCOTIA "REBELLION" the Americans gave up their schemes to woo the remaining British colonies over to their cause. They began a campaign of "privateering," aimed at disrupting the commerce and trade of the Loyalist Colonies which included Newfoundland. By 1778 Yankee Privateers were striking regularly at Nova Scotia shipping along the American seaboard, and making daring raids on Nova Scotian ports. To protect the ports of Newfoundland, the military on station saw the need for a home guard to combat the threat.

That year, the military commander at St. John's, Captain Robert Pringle, began work to fortify the town against privateer attacks or a possible invasion. The Americans had tried it at Quebec, at Nova Scotia and Pringle believed there was no reason they would not attempt an invasion of the isolated island colony. Pringle, who was with the Royal Engineers, did not wait for either permission, or help, from England to begin his work. He enlisted a company of workmen and tradesmen whom he called the Newfoundland Companies of Artificers and Labourers and put them to work preparing the town.[1]

He hurried to complete the work on Fort Townshend, which had been begun in 1775, and began work on Military

Road to connect the new fort with "old" Fort William near the head of the harbour. He also started work on a road up the steep slopes of Signal Hill to access the batteries on its summit.[2]

By the following year, the home government was convinced that Pringle's fears and preparations were well warranted. Although the colonial capital itself had not been attacked, several smaller outports on the Avalon peninsula in Conception and Trinity Bays had been raided by the Yankee Privateers.

In 1779, Pringle was granted permission to form a defensive force to be called His Majesty's Newfoundland Regiment of Foot. The Captain was promoted to the rank of Major and also commissioned to raise a company of militia to back up his new Regiment. Major Pringle enlisted 300 men into his new regiment and raised 350 volunteers to serve in his militia. He moved his new Newfoundland Regiment into his new Fort Townshend, which, although not quite finished was complete enough to be occupied and defended.

Nfld. Military Museum

Soldier of His Majesty's Newfoundland Regiment of Foot (Pringle's) which served in Newfoundland in the last years of the American Revolution, 1780-1783.

The threat to the island colony became even more real in 1780 when the French joined the American War of Independence on the side of

New England colonials. Rumours spread rapidly that the Americans and their new-found allies were planning an invasion of Newfoundland.

The garrisons at St. John's and in the more strategic outports were strengthened in anticipation of the attack but it did not materialize. The reinforced Royal Navy squadron on station in the colony did an admirable job of keeping American Privateers from attacking Newfoundland settlements in the remaining three years of the war, sinking or capturing forty of them with the loss of only three ships to themselves.[3]

With the end of the American Revolutionary War in 1783 and the signing of peace between England and France and the new Republic of the United States of America, the military installations in Newfoundland were downgraded and Pringle's Royal Newfoundland Regiment was disbanded. Ten years of peace followed, then in 1793 with the outbreak of the French Revolution, England found itself once again at war with France.

In charge of the military at St. John's was Captain Thomas Skinner of the Royal Engineers, and he immediately petitioned England to send him resources to beef up the defences of the colony because he feared that French could, and would, strike at British possessions in North America, including the island of Newfoundland. Captain Skinner was so convinced of the possibility of attack that he did not wait for help from England. He raised four companies of volunteers at St. John's which he named the Royal Newfoundland Volunteers and personally paid for its expenses out of his own pocket.

For a year Skinner's petitions seemed to fall on deaf ears, and it was a domestic incident not a foreign threat that finally drew the attention of the home government to the situation in the colony.

In the fall of 1794, Royal Navy warships in Newfoundland were ordered to rendezvous for a voyage to Spain, where they were to join the fleet in action against the French. One of the ships, H.M.S. *Boston,* was undermanned and its Captain sent one of its Lieutenants ashore to "press-gang" enough men to bring the ship's crew up to its full complement. The officer, Lt. Lawrey, while in the pursuit of his duty was murdered by a gang of men who resisted him and the incident resulted in a great deal of uneasiness between the military and the citizenry of the town.

Colonel Skinner's reports of the affair probably prompted the home government to finally listen to his petitions for help for the colony.

In the spring of 1795, King George III granted Captain Skinner permission to form a company of Fencibles, or infantry, to officially be called the Royal Newfoundland Regiment of Foot. Skinner was promoted to the rank of Colonel and commissioned to enlist officers and ensigns from the military companies already on station, and from the general population of St. John's and the outports; "...such gentlemen as were likely, from their locality, responsibility and influence, soon to raise the quotas of men required for their respective commissions."[4]

Colonel Skinner promoted and appointed officers from his own Corps of Engineers and from the 2nd Battalion Royal Artillery, who were also on station at St. John's, to his new Regiment, and hand picked prominent citizens from the town to be his ensigns.

Skinner's Adjutant, a former N.C.O. in the Royal Artillery, his Quartermaster and his Sergeant-Major were sent out to him from England to help him whip his new Regiment into shape. The Royal Newfoundland Regiment of Foot was to

Soldier of Skinner's Regiment

have a complement of 600 men. The Governor of the colony, William Waldegrave, considered the logistics of housing and feeding such a large company of soldiers in a town whose population was about 3,000 during the cold winter months to be a cause for concern. He wrote the Secretary of the Home Department, the Duke of Portland, requesting him "to order provisions to be sent out to them (R.N.R.) as soon as possible...as provisions are scarce and buying them at St. John's might distress the inhabitants."[5]

Recruitment for the regiment began at the end of September, after the fishing season had ended and the "dieters," or seasonal fishermen, had departed for England. By December, more than half the complement of the Regiment had been enlisted, and recruitment continued throughout the winter of 1795-96. But before the Regiment ever began its training it was put to work as labourers.

During the winter, Col. Skinner put his Regiment to work preparing the defenses of St. John's. He had a blockhouse, barracks, and battery of guns erected on Signal Hill, the heavy cannon being hoisted by ropes from the sea below up the steep cliffs of the hills. He installed batteries at Fort Frederick (Pancake Rock), Fort Waldegrave (Chain Rock), and Fort Amherst at the entrance to the "Narrows" on the South Side Hills. At each of the batteries or "Forts," he also built shot heating furnaces to ensure that each location was always supplied with ammunition.[6]

That winter the barracks at Fort Townshend were not big enough to accommodate the new members of the Regiment so Skinner had them billeted out into private housing around the town. Work went on at Fort Townshend to complete it and Fort William was renovated and enlarged as much as it could be within its existing ramparts.

By the spring of 1796 most of the work had been completed on the fortifications of the town but barracks for the soldiers at Fort Townshend still had not been finished. Those of the Regiment already billeted there were greatly overcrowded.[7] Skinner billeted the rest of the Regiment under canvas in the parade square of the fort and began their military training.

To train and drill the "new" Regiment, Skinner called on the "old" soldiers of the Royal Nova Scotia Regiment which had been sent to Newfoundland the previous year in a faint-hearted show of defence for the island colony. The Royal Nova Scotia Regiment was made up largely of older "refugee" soldiers from the New England colonies who had remained loyal to the crown during the American Revolution. Many of them "were well disciplined non-commissioned officers, and were of great service in drilling and forming the young recruits of the Royal Newfoundland Regiment; and it was astonishing how soon the latter became fit for duty."[8]

Throughout the spring and summer the Newfoundlanders were trained and drilled and by August were showing enough skill and discipline that their "old soldier" instructors were recalled to their home base in Nova Scotia. Augmented by the 2nd Battalion Royal Artillery and a few companies of militia Britain's oldest colony and its newest

Regiment were on their own.

Governor Waldegrave, Colonel Skinner, and even the townspeople were all feeling very proud and satisfied with their efforts, and as one observer put it; "a wish seemed to be inspired that something might happen to test the fidelity of the whole."[9] If they did wish for such an opportunity they didn't have long to wait. On the morning of September 1st, 1796 an alarm was given from the guns on Signal Hill. Ships flying the tri-colours of Revolutionary France were heading towards the narrows of St. John's harbour.

About one dozen French warships under command of Rear-Admiral Richery had arrived once again to invade Britain's oldest colony. Richery had 1,500 troops aboard his invasion fleet which consisted of his flagship *La Jupitor* of seventy-four guns, six other ships of the line, two frigates, and two or three smaller warships or transport vessels.

Governor James Wallace at once declared martial law. He rallied the troops at the forts and batteries, and the Royal Navy ships in the harbour which consisted of his flagship of fifty-four guns, two frigates, and a sloop-of-war. He ordered all able-bodied men of the town "—merchants with their domestic and wharf establishments, Captains of vessels with their crews, planters with their fishermen and sharemen—" to assemble on the parade ground at Fort Townshend.[10]

There, he pressed them all into service, sending some to man the batteries and forts around the town, and the rest to the heights of Signal Hill and the South Side Hills. All that day the Governor scurried to ready his defences. In actual fact he was running a huge bluff, hoping it would work. The civilians sent to man the hills around the narrows were made to march back and forth along the crests of the hills in military formations to convince the French that the town was defended by a large garrison.

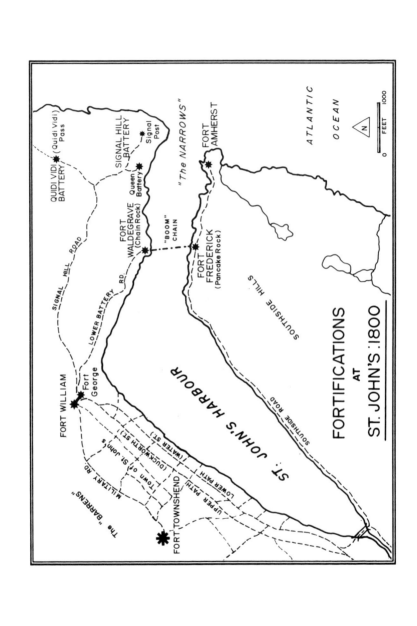

FORTIFICATIONS
AT
ST. JOHN'S : 1800

QUIDI VIDI BATTERY (Quidi Vidi) Pass

SIGNAL HILL BATTERY

Signal Post

Queen Battery

FORT WALDEGRAVE (Chain Rock)

"The NARROWS"

FORT AMHERST

ATLANTIC OCEAN

FEET

"BOOM" CHAIN

FORT FREDERICK (Pancake Rock)

SIGNAL HILL ROAD

LOWER BATTERY RD.

SOUTHSIDE HILLS

FORT WILLIAM

Fort George

SOUTHSIDE ROAD

ST. JOHN'S HARBOUR

MILITARY RD.

Town of St. John's

(DUCKWORTH ST.)

(WATER ST.)

UPPER PATH

LOWER PATH

The "BARRENS"

FORT TOWNSHEND

In actual fact, Wallace had no more than about 600 regular troops; the Companies of the Royal Newfoundland Regiment, eighty-two men of the Royal Artillery—who were the only battle experienced men under his command-an undermanned company of fifty-two Royal Newfoundland Volunteers, and a handful of marines and sailors from the four warships in the harbour.[11] If he was running a bluff it appeared to work. All that day the French warships stood off the narrows making no attempt to enter and aside from sending flag signals between their ships showed no sign of activity.

Governor Wallace sent scouting parties north and south along the rugged hills to guard against any attempted landing by the French above or below the town. He also had the boom chain across the narrows between Pancake Rock and Chain Rock hauled up from the bottom—a time consuming and difficult chore as three schooners had to use their anchors to drag the chain from the bottom. The schooners were then anchored to the boom and filled with explosives to be used as fire ships if the French should try to force the narrows.[12]

Whatever the reason for the French fleets hesitancy Wallace decided to take full advantage of it and further push his ruse. As evening came on he had all the tents at Fort Townshend struck and packed up to Signal Hill where under cover of darkness he had them pitched in a long column across the crest of the lofty summit. He also moved cannons, ammunition and supplies up the hill during the night and when dawn broke on the morning of September 2nd, the French were awakened to a sobering sight.

The hilltops were spiked with what seemed to be hundreds of field tents and throngs of men—seemingly thousands—who were marching in long lines continuously along

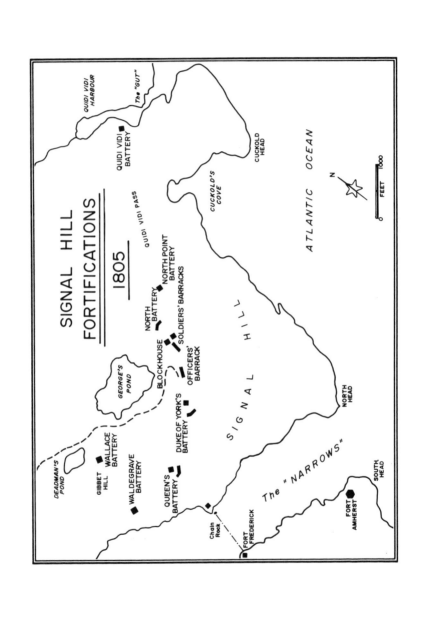

SIGNAL HILL
FORTIFICATIONS

1805

QUIDI VIDI HARBOUR
The "GUT"
QUIDI VIDI BATTERY
CUCKOLD HEAD
CUCKOLD'S COVE
ATLANTIC OCEAN
QUIDI VIDI PASS
NORTH POINT BATTERY
NORTH BATTERY
SOLDIERS' BARRACKS
BLOCKHOUSE
OFFICERS' BARRACK
GEORGE'S POND
DUKE OF YORK'S BATTERY
SIGNAL HILL
NORTH HEAD
WALLACE BATTERY
DEADMAN'S POND
GIBBET HILL
WALDEGRAVE BATTERY
QUEEN'S BATTERY
The "NARROWS"
SOUTH HEAD
Chain Rock
FORT FREDERICK
FORT AMHERST
N
FEET 1000

the crests of the hills. Richery could only have thought the town of St. John's was a veritable fortress.

Again the French fleet stood off all day, frantically flourishing signals among themselves. On the morning of September 3rd, they made their first move to test the defences of the narrows. A couple of the warships began tacking towards the harbour but when a couple of cannon shots from the Fort Amherst battery told the Frenchmen that they were well within range of the town's defenses they quickly retreated. The enemy fleet continued to stand off all that day and the next morning finally withdrew southwards without having made any serious attempt to be the last French invasion of British territory in North America.[13]

The sudden appearance of the French invasion fleet convinced Governor Wallace and Colonel Skinner that St. John's should be even more fortified. This time they had run a bluff and it had worked. The next time they might not be so fortunate. All the harbour batteries were secured and a completely new group of fortifications were constructed on Signal Hill, which it was decided would be the main redoubt for the garrison of Newfoundland.

In the fall of 1796 work began on a blockhouse, barracks, a powder magazine, a storehouse and seven additional gun batteries atop the hill. Two batteries which had been allowed to fall into disrepair at Quidi Vidi Pass and Quidi Vidi gut were also repaired and refortified.[14]

No further threat to the old town of St. John's or any other outport of the island colony from the French materialized throughout the winter of 1796-97, but in the spring of the following year the Royal Newfoundland Regiment and the colony it guarded would find themselves once again threatened, and once again the threat would come from within, not from without.

R.N.R. PROFILE; OLD ST. JOHN'S — MILITARY PAWN

The old town of St. John's, today the oldest European built city in North America, has a history of over 400 years, and for more than half that time the town was a military pawn in a prolonged chess game played out to determine who would rule the vast, rich continent of North America. It became a battleground for France and England: was captured and recaptured, ransomed and ransacked, plundered and burned, yet it and its determined people persevered.

St. John's, almost from the time of the discovery of its superb, natural harbour, became important to the colonial powers of Europe who wanted to exploit the bountiful fishery off the coasts of the rugged island of Newfoundland. The Spanish, Portuguese, French, and English all vied to control it. By 1580 only the French and English continued to contest ownership of the island and over the next two hundred years would fight, almost regularly, over its ownership.

The English finally established themselves on the north and east coasts of the island and made the harbour of St. John's, and the town that grew up around it their "official" capital of the new-found colony. To defend it they began to build fortifications, which at first were simple and crude, and poorly armed and defended. They proved no defence at all against the French who three times attacked, sacked and burned the old town between 1696 and 1709.

The first attack came as a complete surprise to the garrison and townspeople of St. John's in the bitterly cold winter of 1696-97. On January 20th, a French force of 400 regulars, courier de bois and Indians from Quebec under command of Pierre LeMoyne Sieur d'Iberville, surprised the sleeping town after an overland march from Placentia. They quickly captured the town and most of its citizens. A few dozen escaped to the safety of the old fort in the town and spent three days being threatened and harangued by the French who could not attack because their cannon were bogged down in snow drifts a few miles south of the town. D'Iberville finally decided to terrorize the fort into submission by having the Indians scalp one of the townspeople and sending him; blood streaming down his face into the fort with the message that if its defenders did not surrender, all inside would be treated to the same fate.[15]

The fort surrendered and after plundering and looting the town for three weeks, d'Iberville loaded his booty and prisoners which he intended to ransom, put the old town to the torch, and returned to the French headquarters at Placentia.

The town of St. John's was a little better prepared for the next French attack, or at least the military garrison there was. In January of 1705, a mixed force of 450 French and Indians once again marched overland from Placentia to attack the town. At dawn on January 22nd, they surged into the town indiscriminately killing men, women and children alike. This time Fort William held out once again, and despite threats, bombardments and the intimidating sight of a young child whose throat had been slit by the Indians, its commander, Lieutenant John Moody, refused to surrender.[16]

After a six week siege, the French could still not dislodge the stubborn Moody from the fort, and as spring approached, so too would the threat of English reinforcements. The French commander, Monsieur de Subercase, loaded his plunder, 300 prisoners he would ransom, put the town to the firebrand for the second time in seven years, and sailed away. Although he had killed over 30 settlers and fishermen and done over £150,000 worth of damage to the English colonial capital and its fishery, he had not succeeded in destroying the

English presence on the island, having left Fort William intact.

Four years passed before the French once again attempted to destroy the British fishery on the island and force them to quit their colony. Just before Christmas, 1708, Sieur de St. Ovide de Brouillan left Placentia with a French-Indian force of 164 men and marched on the old British colonial town. This time, the fort would be taken before the town, thus ensuring victory. De Brouillan and his men reached the snow-piled palisades of the fort just before midnight on New Year's Eve, 1708.

As the celebrating English soldiers rang in the New Year with a chorus of "Auld Lange Syne" the French climbed the walls and were quickly among the partying redcoats. The capture took less than half an hour, and as the New Year broke on the old town of St. John's, its defences, and the fate of the entire colony was in the hands of the French conquerors. This time however, the old town did not suffer the same fate as it had in its previous conquests.

Instead of being ransacked and burned, the town and its defences were ransomed back to the British by a miffed de Brouillan, who had entertained visions of becoming governor of the British colonial capital, after he had been ordered to destroy and burn it and return to Placentia.[17]

As the war for possession of North America heated up, the British took the defence of St. John's, and the fishery of the colony of Newfoundland, much more seriously. They reinforced and expanded their principal battery of defence, Fort William. Its ramparts were faced with brick and the parapets were bomb-proofed. More barracks for more soldiers were built and the old fort even boasted a chapel.

Smaller batteries at the mouth of the harbour's "narrows" were also reinforced. By 1750, St. John's was garrisoned by four companies of the 40th Regiment of Foot, numbering 350 men, and by a company of fifty men of the Royal Artillery. Their defences were dispersed in three forts around the town and harbour. Fort William was armed with seven 24-pounders, six 18-pounders and ten 5-pounders. Fort George, situated just below the main fort was armed with thirteen 24-pounders and ten light cannon. The "Castle," or Fort Frederick, on the south side of the "narrows" mounted four 18-pounders.

Despite this apparent, adequate arsenal of defence, it was no deterrent to the French who again attacked, invaded and captured the town of St. John's in 1762; once again by an attack overland rather than by sea. The British recaptured it after a hard fought battle which saw them storm the heights of Signal Hill, then pound the captured Fort William below them into submission after three days of cannon fire in September.[18]

The British then decided, as the French had so graphically demonstrated to them, that Fort William was not defensible against a land force that commanded the summit of Signal Hill. Accordingly, construction was begun on a new fort on a commanding site on the west side of the harbour, well out of range of any guns that might be brought to play on it from the harbour or the hill. Named Fort Townshend, building went slowly at first but was quickly speeded up when the American Revolutionary war broke out in 1776. Forts William, George and Frederick, as well as the batteries at the narrows and atop Signal Hill were also refortified and rearmed.

Drained of all British regular Army troops, Newfoundland was left to its own defences for its self-defence. In 1779, Capt. Robert Pringle was granted permission to raise a defensive force of foot and a local company of militia. He succeeded in raising 650 men for the defence of the colony and hurriedly completed work on the new Fort Townshend. But the attack the Newfoundlanders feared from the Americans never came and with the peace of 1783, Pringle's defences at St. John's were downgraded. Ten years of peace followed during which the forts of St. John's were once again allowed to fall into disrepair.

With the outbreak of war between England and France in 1793, the colony of Newfoundland found itself again responsible for its own defence. With no real help from England, the colony struggled to build up its defences from its own resources and population, fearing the French would once again attempt an invasion of the colony. The skeleton military guard in the old colonial capital proved to be right when in September of 1796 a large French fleet appeared off the narrows of St. John's harbour and threatened to attack the town for three days.

A brave bluff, run by the then Governor, James Wallace, who made a great show of making only hundreds of men look like thousands, convinced the French that the town was too heavily defended for them to assault it. The French fleet sailed away, and the British scurried to seriously fortify their island colony.[19]

Resources and reinforcements arrived to strengthen the old town and its defences. All the town's and harbour batteries were refurbished and a completely new group of fortifications were constructed on Signal Hill, which it was decided would be the main redoubt for the garrison of Newfoundland. In the fall of 1796 work began on a blockhouse, several barracks, a powder magazine, a storehouse and seven additional gun batteries atop Signal Hill. Two batteries which had been allowed to fall into disrepair at Quid Vidi Pass and Quidi Vidi "Gut" were also repaired and refortified.[20]

No further threat to the colony from the French materialized throughout the Napoleonic wars of the late eighteenth
and early nineteenth centuries, largely due to the realization
by the British after more than 100 years, their isolated island
colony with its bountiful fishery was coveted by other, powerful nations who had long ago recognized the riches that
could be wrought from its fog-shrouded shores.

Endnotes:

1. O'Flaherty, Maj. John P.; "The Royal Newfoundland Regiment." *Book of Newfoundland,* Vol. IV. p. 351.

2. O'Neill, Paul; *The Oldest City,* p. 95. The Home government did not seem to be pleased with Pringle's initiative to do the "King's works" in Newfoundland. When Pringle asked for pay for his Companies of Artificers and Labourers, all he received to pay the men for their year's labour was three pounds for each Artificer, and forty shillings for each Labourer.

3. Webber, David; "The Military History of St. John's." *Book of Newfoundland* Vol. VI. p. 532.

4. Prowse; op. cit., p. 368.

5. O'Neill; *The Oldest City,* p. 96.

6. Prowse; op, cit., p. 368-369.

7. At one point, conditions were so crowded at the forts that the soldiers slept three to a bunk. It can only be imagined what such conditions resulted in. On one occasion a soldier at one of the forts was tried for sodomy, claiming in his defence that he was dreaming of a beautiful girl at the time. He was hanged a few days later for his "unnatural crime." O'Neill; *The Oldest City,* p. 96.

8. Prowse; op. cit., p. 368.

9. Ibid.

10. Ibid.

11. Webber; op. cit., p. 533.

12. Fardy, B.D.; *Under Two Flags,* p. 126-127.

13. Fardy; op. cit., p. 128. Admiral Richery vented his frustration on the tiny town of Bay Bulls just south of St. John's. He landed there on the 4th of September taking the whole town prisoner. He questioned some of the inhabitants about the strength of St. John's, and one of them told him that the town was garrisoned by at least 5,000 troops. The Frenchman doubted his veracity but could not break the man down. Against such heavy odds, Richery knew even an invasion of St. John's overland would not be successful. He burned the town of Bay Bulls to the ground on September 5th and took 82 of the inhabitants prisoner and left Newfoundland waters, unsuccessful in his bid to be the last invader of Britain's oldest colony.

14. Webber; op. cit., p. 533.

15. Rutledge, Joseph L.; *Century of Conflict.* p. 162

16. Fardy, B.D.; *Under Two Flags.* p. 76-77.

17. See endnote number 2.

18. Fardy, B.D.; "Signal Hill; Last Battle For Canada." *Great Stories From The Canadian Frontier.* p. 21-28.

19. Prowse; op. cit., p. 370.

20. Webber; op. cit., p. 533.

Chapter Four

Rebellion and Dishonour

HE THREAT OF A FRENCH INVASION OF ST. JOHN'S and the colony of Newfoundland in the late summer of 1796, served to draw the inhabitants of the old town, both civilian and military together in a united effort to resist a foreign foe. But the feeling of "togetherness" dissipated as soon as the threat did. The old feelings of animosity between the Irish population and the British authorities which became dangerously apparent during the Lt. Lawery incident in 1794 began to surface once again.

In May of 1797, the Royal Navy warship H.M.S. *Latona* arrived on station in Newfoundland. As the summer wore on it was learned by some members of the Royal Newfoundland Regiment garrison that the sailors were planning a mutiny to force better treatment from the Admiralty. The mutiny was to occur in St. John's at the same time that the other ships in port in England would also rise in revolt.

On August 3rd, the crew of the *Latona* made their move to mutiny but the officers and marines of the warship quickly quashed the attempt and restored order. The newly appointed Governor of the colony, Admiral William Waldegrave, threatened the mutineers with dire consequences if any further attempts were made. The rebellious seamen, however, were not ready to give up their struggle.

St. John's shortly after the Battle of Signal Hill showing the harbour and the "narrows" with Signal Hill (third rise) and Gibbet Hill (second rise) at left. On the right side of the narrows (background) is Fort Amherst, built soon after the recapture of the town in 1762. It was the first real effort of the British to properly fortify the entrance to the harbour.

On August 8th, some of the sailors of the *Latona* met with a sergeant of the Royal Newfoundland Regiment named James Dailey, under some fish flakes in a cove in St. John's harbour. Sgt. Dailey told the sailors that the Regiment would be willing to join in their mutiny and together they could seize control of the town and force the authorities to comply with their demands.

Sgt. Dailey told the seamen that their own living conditions were as bad as the Navy's and discipline as harsh, if not harsher, than that of the Admiralty. In fact, the reason for revolt among the ranks of the Royal Newfoundland Regiment was more deep rooted than merely the wretched living conditions of the soldiers. The sailors returned to their ship more resolved than ever to complete their plan but a few days later they learned that the coincidental mutinies that were to take place in home ports in England had failed and the ringleaders hanged.

Most of the would-be mutineers realized that their plan was foiled and a few malcontents or die-hards put the blame for their failure on the shoulders of the men of the Royal Newfoundland Regiment whose help had not materialized.

On August 12th, Sgt. Dailey was identified as the soldier who had met with the plotting sailors and in his defence claimed that he did not recall what he had said because he was too drunk, having imbibed a full flask of brandy that evening. Governor Waldegrave, already outraged over the *Latona* incident, became incensed at the revelation of this latest act of treason among his own ranks. He wanted to hang Sgt. Dailey and the leaders of the *Latona* mutiny on the spot but his commission did not allow him to conduct court martials.

Soon, word of the possible uprising of the whole military forces in the town spread among the general population who

became very panicky and fearful. To allay their apprehen-
sions, Waldegrave invited the whole town to a reassuring
ceremony at the Court House where they witnessed Private
Dailey — for he had been busted to the ranks by Colonel
Skinner — take the oath of allegiance to the Crown in the
presence of all the town's magistrates and military officers.
Private Dailey was then thrown into the guardhouse at Fort
Townshend to await transport to England where he would
be tried for treason.[1]

The fate of Sgt. Dailey did nothing to relieve the rebellious feelings of the Irish soldiers in the Newfoundland
Regiment. During the winter of 1797-98, as living conditions
became worse for the men at the forts and batteries around
the town, the mood for mutiny became more manifest.

Many of the Irish recruits of the Regiment, whether from
the mother country or Newfoundland born, were in sympathy with, or were members of the U.I.S. (United Irishmen
Society) which had been founded in Ireland in 1791. The
Society had as its aim an end to the oppressive rule of the
English in Ireland. In Newfoundland, the movement found
many supporters among the Irish born population of St.
John's, and the villages of the "southern shore" along the east
coast of the Avalon Peninsula.

Many of them had sworn an oath of allegiance to the
cause, and some of the soldiers had formed "cells" within
their companies in the Regiment. Like their kin, they felt they
were being subjected to the same oppression by their English
overseers as their forbearers were in Ireland. One observer
comments; "...the poor living conditions of the troops, the
near slavery of the fishermen and labourers who were kept in
debt by their employers year after year, the denial of religious and political freedom, the laws which forbade the free
movement of the inhabitants, and a host of other pieces of

legislation which made any change of betterment of the poor 'impossible',"[2] all contributed to the mood of the Irish in Newfoundland.

The "cell" soldiers of the U.I.S. movement within the Regiment were probably worse off than the civilians. As the winter of 1797-98 closed in, the soldiers again found themselves facing miserable conditions. Barracks at the forts and batteries were still overcrowded or unfinished and morale was low. On October 2nd, the first food stores were issued to the troops, and it was found that the salt pork and flour — the staples of the soldiers' diet — were largely spoiled.

Out of about 1,500 pounds of salt pork less than 300 were fit for human consumption, and over a ton of barrelled flour was so rotten it had to be thrown into the harbour. Colonel Skinner reported that a man "peeled the skin off two pieces (of the salt pork) and thrust his fingers into the meat which I believe could not have been the case with sound meat; nearly all pieces were quite yellow."[3]

The spoiled food could not be replaced by the commissary so late in the year and the military was forced to buy or requisition food from the townspeople. This led to further resentment on the part of the inhabitants towards the British authorities, and added fuel to the smouldering fires of rebellion among the Irish faction of the Royal Newfoundland Regiment. By January of 1798, all the available food stores for the Regiment had been tapped and the soldiers were down to about ten weeks supply of rations. The garrisons went on short issues in the hope that their meagre supplies would see them through to the spring when supply ships would begin to arrive from England.

To add to the soldiers' misery, a fire broke out at Fort William about 2:30 A.M. on the morning of March 24, 1798. The blaze swept through the old fort quickly, destroying all

FORT WILLIAM: Constructed between 1697 and 1700, the fort was military headquarters of the Royal Newfoundland Regiment and others until 1775. During that time the "old" fort was three times attacked and captured by French forces.

of the officers barracks and a half dozen of the soldiers' barracks. All of the medical supplies, most of the provisions, and all of the hoarded foodstores at the fort were also lost. The whole fort might have gone up in flames had it not been for the efforts of the crews of the Royal Navy ships in the harbour and the townspeople.

As it was the dead of winter no timber was readily available for repairs to the barracks; and the freezing weather precluded them from being billeted outside in tents. The burned-out soldiers were forced to "shack-up" with already overcrowded bunkmates. The smouldering resentments of the soldiers continued to be fanned as the spring of 1798 approached.

The first ships from England carrying the much needed food supplies for the town and garrisons of the old town also brought news of conditions in the home towns of many of the Irish inhabitants and soldiers of the Regiment. It was not good, and the local factions of the U.I.S. began making public grumblings of unrest.

By the time Governor Waldegrave returned to his post in Newfoundland, all hell had broken loose in Ireland. The United Irishmen Society had risen in bloody revolt against British rule in several countries. Although short-lived, the

Rebellion of 1798 was a bloody affair that saw some 30,000 of the "rebels" killed by British troops who committed some calculated atrocities against the soldier "rebels" and their civilian supporters.[4]

With this news in his possession, the Governor worked worriedly and frantically to keep the peace in his isolated colony. He wrote the Duke of Portland in England, requesting that he order the Chief Justice for Newfoundland, D'Ewes Coke, to take up permanent residence in St. John's, because, as Waldegrave put it; "nine-tenths of the inhabitants of the Island are either natives of Ireland or immediate descendants from them, and that the whole of those are of Roman Catholic persuasion." The Governor further stated; "...it is therefore to the wise and vigilant administration of the civil power that we must look to preserve peace and good order...in this settlement."[5]

It was impossible for Waldegrave to suppress this news from Ireland for long and given the discontent already prevailing among the Irish in the town, particularly that of his own soldiers, the Governor took some desperate measures. Some of them appeared soothing, while others were even more inflammatory.

He courted the favour of the first Catholic Bishop of the colony, Dr. James O'Donel. The Bishop was known to have a revulsion of "mob rule," which he equated with the French Revolution, and did all he could to pacify the disgruntled Irish population of St. John's, including the hapless soldiers of the Regiment. O'Donel, it was reported, "was pleased to see companies of the volunteers, headed by their Protestant officers coming to the chapel to be instructed in the duties of religion and loyalty."[6]

This calculated strategy of Waldegrave seemed to have the desired effect, but another, aimed solely at the discipline of the soldiers served only to exacerbate the situation. He posted orders that curbed the few earthly pleasures that made the miserable lives of the soldiers tolerable. He forbid the men to frequent the taverns and "bawdy houses" of the town and ordered that the men could no longer keep pets at the forts, which was a favoured pastime of many who found it broke up the tedium and boredom of daily routine. Waldegrave's written orders stated; "all dogs straggling about the fort after Gun Fire are to be bayoneted by the sentinels or hanged by the Guard."[7]

The Governor's harsh discipline and clergy alliances managed to keep peace in the colony during the summer and fall of 1798, despite the horrific news of the Irish Rebellion which kept funnelling into the town. When Waldegrave left the colony that autumn, he felt he had a firm clamp on any thoughts of rebellion harboured by the townspeople and soldiers, and left firm orders with his military lieutenants of how to deal with any grumblings within the ranks of the Royal Newfoundland Regiment.

Throughout the winter of 1798-99, the strict discipline and harsh conditions of the Regiment did not improve, nor did the situation of the Irish inhabitants. The U.I.S. increased its pressure to incite open revolt among the Irish citizenry and soldiers but the severity of the Newfoundland winter took precedence over any political philosophy.

Despite the strict discipline and harsh punishments doled out to the Regiment's members, the winter of 1798-99 saw twenty-two men desert its ranks. Most of the deserters were aided by sympathetic civilians who were members of the U.I.S. and ferreted them away to the small villages of the "southern shore" whose populations were almost entirely of Irish descent. These civilians too ran a high risk. Any of them caught aiding deserters were threatened with a whipping or hanging, and a reward of 80 shillings was offered to any person who turned in, or informed on, any of the army deserters.[8]

In the comfortable drawing rooms and legislative halls of London however, politicians and military governors were preparing their final plans to keep the lid on the dissention in their far off colony of Newfoundland. Whether it was a deliberate, calculated affront to the Irish populations of St. John's — both citizen and soldier — or a desperate attempt by the authorities to intimidate them, London officials installed Brigadier-General William Skerrett as commanding officer of the Royal Newfoundland Regiment. Skerrett had, as a Colonel, headed a force known as "Skerrett's Horse" against the "rebels" in the Irish Rebellion the year before, and was noted for the brutal and efficient fashion in which he had carried out his orders.

Skerrett arrived in Newfoundland in the spring of 1799 with Governor Waldegrave. He wasted no time in tightening discipline at the garrisons, and issued stern warnings to the townspeople as well. His fervour and his record served to only further determine the zealots of revolt among the U.I.S. to open rebellion. However, they had learned a valuable lesson from the attempted mutiny by the crew of the H.M.S. *Latona* a few years earlier. The Royal Navy was on station in force, as well as the Governor and his officers who seemed well prepared for any attempt at revolt.

The would-be "rebels" of St. John's decided that the best time for their rebellion would be early in the spring before the Governor returned from his "season" in England, and shipping — including the reappearance of the Royal Navy — began to arrive in the colony.

As the winter of 1799-80 progressed, the regression of the town's inhabitants grew worse. More and more restrictions were placed on the citizenry and the dual harshness of the winter and isolation contributed to their discontent. Some of the militant insurrectionists of the colony took action. The latest restriction placed on the inhabitants was decreed by Lt. Governor Skerrett in the winter of the year. It was a by-law forbidding the people from allowing their hogs to roam free in the streets of the town, and threatening the owners with fines or confiscation of their livestock. In an isolated town where food always ran short during the long winter months, the law was viewed very seriously.

Late in February 1800, some persons unknown posted up leaflets around the town "threatening the persons and property of the magistrates if they insisted in enforcing (the) proclamation." Skerrett offered a reward of 100 guineas for the apprehension of the people responsible for the threatening handbills, and concerned merchants offered 200 guineas more. Although it was a considerable amount in such hard times, nobody came forward with any information.[9]

The incident raised more real concern among the authorities in the town, and later that winter they learned that their fears were well founded. Early in April, news that there was an actual plan to revolt by the citizens and the military was brought to the Lt. Governor by a special source. Bishop O'Donel, whose favour had been cultivated by Governor Waldegrave, leaked the information to Skerrett. The Bishop is reported to have heard of the plot from an Irishwoman in her "confession" whose husband was involved in it. Governor Waldegrave's liaison with the Irish Catholics seemed to have paid off.

The planned revolt was set to occur in late April, before the arrival of the Royal Navy squadron, the Governor, and possibly fresh troops from England. The U.I.S. "cells" within the Royal Newfoundland Regiment were to take the lead in the uprising which would see the general population join in upon their taking the initiative. Men from the three main garrisons in the town, at Signal Hill, Fort William and Fort Townshend, planned to desert their posts with their arms and rendezvous behind a powder shed at Fort Townshend.[10]

The leader of the mutinous soldiers was one Sergeant Kelly who had enlisted from forty to fifty men of the Regiment to follow him. Kelly had been told by a civilian member of the U.I.S. movement — James Murphy — that as many as 300-400 of the townspeople were ready to join them in their mutiny.

Forewarned, Lt. Governor Skerrett had instructed all his officers at the forts to be especially vigilant of their troops and not allow them to be idle or form large gatherings. The first hint that the soldiers might indeed be planning a mutiny came on Sunday, April 20th. The normal parade drill was carried out by the soldiers of Fort Townshend, but it was noticed by their commander that it was done in a very careless and undisciplined manner.

Three days later, Captain Thomas Tremblett, in command of the garrison atop Signal Hill, reported six of his troops to Colonel Skinner for lazing about and being "out of uniform," and threw another one in the guardhouse for being drunk on duty. Sergeant Kelly concluded that Capt. Tremblett, or someone, suspected that something was afoot. He met with his prospective mutineers and decided that they could wait no longer. He drew up a hasty plan that would see them desert the following night. Their rendezvous was to be at the place agreed upon at 11:00 P.M. on the night of April 24th.

Sergeant Kelly then had the problem of spreading the word to the other conspirators at Forts William and Townshend, and to Mr. Murphy and the civilian U.I.S. members. It appears that neither Kelly or Murphy had enough time to inform all those who were to join them. Sgt. Kelly, posted at Signal Hill, was to desert with about twenty men, including two sentries who would ensure their escape route and meet up with the other deserters from Fort William and Fort Townshend. He was hoping that the other soldiers who were not committed to the venture would change their minds at the last minute and join the mutiny.

From the beginning, things went wrong for the mutineers. Shortly after dark on the evening of April 24, Sergeant Kelly and twelve men from his barracks, including the guards left their post, taking their arms with them. They were supposed to be joined by a half-dozen others from another battery on the hill, but within minutes of them deserting their posts their absence was discovered by the vigilant Capt. Tremblett and the alarm was raised.

Kelly and his group made it to their rendezvous point at Fort Townshend and joined only six troops from that post. He had expected to meet up with another thirty men. It was later learned that the soldiers at Fort William who had planned to desert had been delayed because of a party which was being held for Colonel Skinner that night, and prevented the would-be mutineers from leaving the fort unnoticed.

Kelly's small company of deserters broke into the powder shed and stole twenty-three stacks of muskets which they intended to arm their arriving comrades, and the expected civilian support. But as the mutineers wasted time waiting, their alerted officers did not. Capt. Tremblett had by now notified Col. Skinner at Fort William and Lt. Governor Skerrett at Fort Townshend. James Murphy either had not had time to rally the civilian "rebels" or they simply backed out of the revolt. By the time Sgt. Kelly realized that no one else would show up it was too late. The town began to swarm with troops running through the streets, and searching houses.

Upon receiving the alarm, Skerrett ordered every officer off duty to assemble all available men to secure the harbour and prevent the escape of the mutineers by sea. He organized pursuit parties and sent them into the woods south and west of the town where Kelly's deserters — for that is all they were now in the face of their failed mutiny — were forced to flee. Skerrett felt sure they would head south for the "southern shore" where they would be given aid by the sympathetic townspeople there.

Sgt. Kelly and his men had by this time dispersed into the woods above St. John's, but the night turned stormy and their pursuers did not get very far when they were forced to return empty handed. The search for the mutineers continued for three days when in the early morning of April 27th, a boy who had been sent back to the town to secure food for the deserters was either apprehended or gave himself up to the authorities. He led Skerrett's troops back to Kelly's camp and a firefight took place in which some of the deserters were wounded, one of them was believed to be Sgt. Kelly as his musket was found stained with blood.[11]

Within two weeks sixteen of the nineteen mutineers had been captured. Besides those taken at the skirmish with Sgt. Kelly, two others later surrendered to the authorities, who, as Skerrett reported, "were absolutely starved." The last one found, although described as a "most dangerous fellow," did not give any resistance when he was found hiding in the loft of the Catholic chapel at Fort William. Some of the captured "rebels" informed on others who had planned to join the mutiny but could not and Skerrett rounded up twenty more soldiers from the Regiment and quickly convened his court martial.

Of the sixteen actual deserters who had mutinied under Sgt. Kelly and had been captured, five were sentenced to be hanged summarily and the other eleven were ordered to be sent to Halifax to be tried for treason by the Duke of Kent, supreme commander of His Majesty's forces in the British colonies of North America. The five men sentenced to death by Skerrett were hanged a few days after their trial on a scaffold erected just behind the powder shed at Fort Townshend where they had tried to complete their mutinous deed.

The other eleven deserters were embarked on a small "schooner," the *Venus*, for transport to Halifax. On route, three of the mutineers, Edward Power, Garrett Fitzgerald, and James Ivony (or Ivany) overpowered the sergeant guarding them and set themselves free. They then overpowered another sergeant-at-arms and his small guard, and succeeded in taking control of the small ship.

The fugitives then made a run for their lives southward for New York. When the *Venus* did not show up on schedule in Halifax the Royal Navy went in pursuit. The soldiers proved to be not very good sailors and they were intercepted and captured by a British man-o-war four days later. Returned to Halifax the fugitives were tried and all of them sentenced to hang for mutiny and treason.

On the morning of July 7, 1800, the citizens of Halifax were witness to a solemn spectacle. The Halifax newspapers, the *Royal Gazette* and the *Nova Scotian Advertiser* recorded the event. The papers reported that "the eleven condemned men, flanked by armed guards and proceeded by a cart draped in black carrying eleven gaping and awaiting black coffins, walked sullenly in slow procession to Fort George, where on Citadel Hill, the gallows were erected. A military band playing the funeral marches accompanied the solemn death parade."[12]

As the men were marched up the gallows steps at the Citadel, late word came that the Duke of Kent had commuted the death sentences of eight of the mutineers, to show, as it was put, the "clemency of His Majesty." The other three, however, Power, Fitzgerald, and Ivony, did not escape the noose, probably because of their attempt to escape in the *Venus*. Only their three heads filled the nooses that morning as the other eight swung empty in the breeze.

Lt. Governor Skerrett was relieved by the news from Halifax of the execution of the three "repeat offender" mutineers but the information he received about Sgt. Kelly's threat and the fact that the leader of the mutiny was still on the loose, worried him intensely.

As soon as he'd quashed the mutiny, Skerrett requested the Duke of Kent to replace the Royal Newfoundland Regiment with a force from Nova Scotia whose loyalty could not be questioned. The Duke had little to send him except for a reassembled Corps of the 6th Regiment Irish Corps known as Pitt's Wild Geese, who had been hurriedly withdrawn from Newfoundland during the Irish Rebellion of 1798. They had been reformed into the 66th Regiment of Foot and now the Duke sent them back to St. John's to replace the Royal Newfoundland Regiment which Skerrett had hurriedly transferred to Nova Scotia, except for two companies who proved their loyalty to the Crown.

On July 2nd, 1800, the Chief Justice of the colony, the Hon. J. Ogden wrote the absent Governor Waldegrave in London outlining his and Skerrett's concerns. He maintained that the threat to the colony was not over, and that he and Skerrett felt that; "Although we are at present without any immediate apprehension of danger, we have no reason to suppose their (the rebels) dispositions have changed, or that their plans of plunder, burning etc. are given up..."[13]

Ogden went on to request a force of 800-1,000 troops from the home government to ensure the security of the colony, which he believed would be in "a state of ferment as it has been and is likely to continue till the business of the union (in Ireland) is settled."[14] He also expressed his reservations about the company of troops that had been sent from Nova Scotia to replace the Royal Newfoundland Regiment, commenting that "they are mostly composed of drafts from the Irish brigades sent three or four years ago to Halifax, of course not so well adapted for the protection required, as a full and complete regiment from England, staunch and well-affected."[15]

With the failure of a general "rising" among the population of the colony, the fears of Ogden and Skerrett were allayed at last. Lt. Governor Skerrett was highly commended for his quick and decisive handling of the mutiny, and for his part, Bishop O'Donel was given great credit by the magistrates, merchants, and principal citizens of the town who petitioned the British government to grant a pension to the clergyman "who along with (Skerrett) was the person who saved the island from becoming a scene of anarchy and confusion."[16]

PROFILE; THE H.M.S. *LATONA* MUTINY OF 1797

The Lt. Lawry press-gang incident at St. John's in 1794 had involved Irishmen, but even in their home country, Englishmen were being press-ganged and shanghaied by the Royal Navy who were in need of crews to man their warships in their latest war with France. By 1797, the press-ganged seamen of the Royal Navy were in a mutinous mood.

In the spring of that year the Royal Navy warship H.M.S. *Latona* of thirty-eight guns arrived in St. John's from England. During the spring and summer the ship lay at anchor in the harbour, the sailors cooped up in what they considered appalling conditions.

Before sailing from England, *Latona's* sailors had plotted with their comrades aboard other vessels to rise in revolt to protest their conditions. They were ordered to sail for Newfoundland, however, before they could put their plan into effect. The ordinary seamen resented the fact that even the marines aboard the ships were treated better than they were. The sailors wanted more pay, better food than the paltry rations they were served — which were often putrid — an end to "press-gangs," and most importantly an end to the excessive punishments that were often meted out to them for trivial offenses by sadistic or tyrannical officers.[17]

Although they sailed from England before they could execute their mutinous plan, the crew of the *Latona* did not abandon it. They waited throughout the summer for word from home ports that the mutiny in the Royal Navy had begun there as planned. While they were at sea on route to Newfoundland the mutiny in England took place and the months they spent at anchor in St. John's harbour waiting for word of it were futile ones.

The mutiny in the Royal Navy had been well planned and co-ordinated, and it erupted at two locations in England simultaneously. At Spithead, a Strait in the English Channel between the Isle of Wight and mainland England, sailors of the Royal Navy fleet assembled there revolted en masse. Negotiations followed between the seamen and the Admiralty and the sailors were successful in having some of their demands met. Satisfied, the Spithead fleet put to sea.

The other mutiny occurred among the ships anchored at the "Nore," an estuary of the Thames River, a safe and favoured harbour of the British fleet. The mutiny at the "Nore" was led by a sailor named Richard Parker, who when approached with the concessions the Spithead mutineers had won, declared that they were not enough and pressed his revolt.

What had started as a revolt within the Royal Navy soon became a lawless rampage that affected the entire vicinity. Sailors of the ships invaded the nearby towns and hamlets looting and robbing and setting up a blockade that cut off the city of London to the seacoast. The lawlessness of the mutineers turned the townspeople, who had been sympathetic to their cause, against the sailors. Officials moved quickly to quell the violence and break the blockade of London. The Royal Marines moved into the area and quickly put down the mutiny, arresting its ringleaders. Court Martials were held and the leader of the affair, Parker, was promptly convicted and hanged from the yardarm of one of the ships in the "Nore."

On the morning of the August 3rd, 1797 the crew of the *Latona* decided it was time to act before they were ordered to sail again. When the ship's officers ordered the fore-topmen aloft they refused to climb the rigging. When Captain Sotheron of the *Latona* threatened punishment for refusing to obey an order, the entire crew challenged him to put them all in irons. Sotheron tried to arrest the leader of the mutiny but the crew resisted, stating that if one of them was to be punished then all of them would have to be. The Captain ordered his officers to draw their swords and the marines to present their bayonets.

A short scuffle ensued in which a few of the sailors, armed only with their knives, were slightly injured by bayonet and sword cuts. After Sotheron controlled the disturbance he immediately sent for the new Governor of the colony, Admiral William Waldegrave. The Governor boarded the *Latona* and took command of the situation, ordering the ringleaders flogged and the entire ship's company to stand by and witness the punishment. When the whipping was finished, Waldegrave delivered a long, harsh and threatening warning to the mutineers. He then told Captain Sotheron and the officers of the *Latona*; "in case any further signs of mutiny should occur among you, do not think of confining the ringleaders but put them to death instantly."[18]

The mutineers did not seem to be intimidated by the Governor's stern lecture or the orders left with the officers of the *Latona*. As Waldegrave later reported; "the language of the seamen afterwards was atrocious. The marines were threatened to be thrown overboard, and 'bloody work' promised as soon as the *Latona* left port."[19]

The crewmen of the *Latona* continued their seditious conspiracy throughout the summer and in August found that they had allies ashore.

On August 8th, sailors from the *Latona* met with a sergeant of the Royal Newfoundland Regiment under a fish flake in one of the harbour's coves. The sergeant told the tars that there were men among the ranks of the Regiment who would be willing to join them in their mutiny. The soldiers' lot too, the sergeant claimed, was as miserable as the sailors. What the soldier did not tell the sailors was that the malcontents among the Royal Newfoundland Regiment had ulterior motives for wanting to join the mutiny. The movement for mutiny among the Regiment was motivated more by politics than practicalities.

Encouraged by the news that they would be joined by the soldiers ashore, the sailors of the *Latona* pressed on with their plan. A few days later, however, they received news that would break the backbone of their conspiracy. A ship arrived from England with newspapers and dispatches for Governor Waldegrave which told of the mutinies at Spithead and the "Nore." The Governor quickly evaluated the news, and concluded that the situation he had on his hands was more serious than he had believed.

The dispatches told him that the mutineers had been put down and that the ringleader at the "Nore" had been hanged. Waldegrave immediately ordered all the companies of the Royal Navy ships ashore for a general address. He turned out the garrisons, including the Royal Newfoundland Regiment to stand by with fixed bayonets while he delivered his speech.

First, Waldegrave complimented the ship's marines for their loyalty, then patronized the other crews who had not yet arisen in revolt. To the crew of the *Latona* his words were pointed and admonishing. He said he hoped that most among them were loyal to their King and country, then went on to say; "but if I am to judge by your conduct, I must think that the majority of you are either villainous or cowards. If the greater number of you are against your officers, and refuse to obey lawful commands, I have a right to say that you are traitors to your King and country. If there are only a few bad men among you, which you pretend to be the case, I maintain that you are a set of dastardly cowards for suffering yourselves to be bullied by a few villains who wish nothing better than to see us become slaves of France."[20]

He gave them a stern warning; "I have given orders to the officers of the Batteries to burn the *Latona* with redhot shot in case you drive me by your mutinous behaviour to that extremity."[21] This of course would mean that the officers of the ship would be killed along with the mutineers, but Waldegrave asserted that those men were willing to sacrifice their lives in the service of their King and country.

Waldegrave then delivered his crowning blow to the mutineers. He read to them the London newspaper accounts of the failed mutiny at the "Nore" and of the fate of its leader Richard Parker. "You were all eager for news and newspapers to see how your great leader, Parker, was coming on. I thank God I have the satisfaction to inform you that he is hanged with many of his atrocious companions."[22] Waldegrave ended with a dire comment, saying he lamented the fact that he did not have the power to convene his own courtmartials for if he did he would have hanged the leader of the *Latona* mutiny.

With the news from home of Parker's death, and the threatening words of Waldegrave's warnings echoing in their heads, the crews of the *Latona* and the other ships returned to their vessels giving up their plans for a general mutiny.

Endnotes:

1. Webber, David A.; *Skinner's Fencibles*; Nfld. Naval and Military Museum - 1964, p. 7.
2. Morris, Don; "Eight Soldiers Met Fate on Gallows After Mutiny." *The Express* Feb. 19, 1992, p. 30.

3. O'Neill; op. cit., p. 100.

4. Newman, Peter R.; *Companion To Irish History: 1603-1921*, p. 134-135. The "Irish Rebellion" of 1798 began on May 23rd of that year in Leinster county and spread throughout the country. Several bloody battles were fought during the summer but the British put down the rebellion quickly and savagely by the end of August, committing some atrocities against the "rebels" and their civilian sympathizers, as well as brutally executing some of the "rebel" leaders.

5. Webber, op. cit., p. 41-42.

6. Harrington, Michael; "United Irishmen's Rising - 1800." *Offbeat History; Evening Telegram*, Jan. 16, 1978.

7. Webber; op. cit., p. 55.

8. O'Neill; *The Oldest City*, p. 100. The harsh discipline imposed on the soldiers of the Regiment during the winter of 1798-99 prompted the desertions. That winter there were reports of sentries on duty atop the heights of Signal Hill who froze to death at their posts.

9. Prowse; op. cit., p. 418.

10. Webber; op. cit., p. 43-44.

11. Harrington; op. cit., Sgt. Kelly was never apprehended just as James Murphy was not. Murphy seems to have disappeared completely, but there were rumours of Kelly's activities and whereabouts long after the attempted rebellion. Five days after the mutiny, Skerrett informed the Duke of Kent in Halifax, that Sgt. Kelly had been seen in Kelligrews, Conception Bay and had been talking with confidence and even impudence, stating that there were at least 200 men sworn into the regiments of Fencibles and Artillery, who were ready to rise at any moment and the "rebellion" was not over yet. There is some speculation that Kelly settled at Kitchuses, Conception Bay, and his descendants survive today.

12. Morris; op. cit., Just before the hangings, the Duke of Kent, supreme commander of His Majesty's forces in North America, and as Morris writes, being an "august person of royal blood, thought it 'proper' to commute the extreme penalty of eight of the Newfoundland soldiers to sentences of life imprisonment."

13. Prowse; op. cit., p. 418.

14. Ibid.

15. Ibid., p. 419.

16. Harrington; op. cit.

17. Punishments dealt out in the Royal Navy at this time were indeed harsh. One sailor was sentenced to receive "six-hundred lashes" for desertion. Another who also deserted was sentenced to 1,000 lashes, and then to be sent "to the Savoy Prison in London to be sent from thence to such places beyond the seas as His Majesty shall think fit, there to serve as a soldier during his natural life." O'Neill; *The Oldest City*, p. 100.

18. See endnote number 1.

19. Morris, Don; "Mutiny on the Waterfront; The *Latona* Misadventure of 1797." *Sunday Express*, June 30, 1991, p. 31.

20. See endnote number 3.

21. O'Neill; *The Oldest City*, p. 99.

22. Prowse; op. cit., p. 373.

Chapter Five

The Call to Arms

HE MUTINY AT ST. JOHN'S in 1800 and the Treaty of Amiens between England and France signed in 1802 dealt a final blow to the existence of the Royal Newfoundland Regiment. What remained of them in Newfoundland was disbanded and those that had been transferred to Nova Scotia were absorbed into other — "more trustworthy" — regular British Army Regiments.[1]

But the death of the Regiment was a short one, and it was resurrected within two years. Only fourteen months after the Treaty of Amiens, England and France were once again at war. Napoleon Bonaparte had seized power in France and threatened to take over all of Europe — including England. All regular British Army Regiments were recalled from their posts in the American colonies and elsewhere to help defend the homeland from Napoleon's threatened invasion. Newfoundland, once again, was left to its own devices to defend itself.

On June 23, 1803, Brigadier-General, John Skerrett, who was still in command of His Majesty's Forces in the colony received orders to raise a regiment of ten companies to be called the Newfoundland Regiment of Fencible Infantry.[2] Skerrett recruited the core of his companies from the veterans of the previous Royal Newfoundland Regiment, and augmented them with men who had previously served with many of the Volunteer and Militia companies that had served in the colony over the past years.

Within eighteen months, Skerrett had his ten companies, consisting of 683 men well trained and drilled and ready to defend the colony. In 1805, permission was granted to Skerrett to officially call his Newfoundland Fencibles, the Royal Newfoundland Regiment. No sooner did Skerrett have his Regiment ready to defend the colony when in 1806 it was loaded aboard five transport vessels and shipped off to Nova Scotia to do duty. It was replaced by the Nova Scotia Fencibles. "This ridiculous exchange," commented one observer, "robbed Brigadier-General Skerrett of 683 trained men acquainted with the area and its problems of defence." Obviously, armed Newfoundlanders were still not to be trusted in their own country.[3]

The Regiment served one year in Halifax, ready to defend the important port against French attack. It soon became obvious however, that Napoleon's difficulties in Europe had not allowed him to attempt an invasion of England and it was highly unlikely he would attempt an attack in America. But if the French couldn't attack, there were others who could. In 1807, the Royal Newfoundland Regiment was sent to Quebec once again, where it did duty as it had over thirty years earlier along the St. Lawrence River, guarding the border with its new American "neighbours" to the south.

There were rumblings south of the border once again and war clouds had begun to gather. In the war between England and France, America had remained neutral, and was content to do so, realizing that its prosperity could greatly increase by carrying on trade with both nations. During the Napoleonic Wars, it appeared to the British that its prosperity was growing too much — at their expense. They still harboured feelings of mistrust towards the young, new nation born out of the fires of rebellion from their own hearth. The Americans' booming trade with European countries, most of whom stood with or under Napoleon, forced the British to act in their own best interest against the Americans.

In 1807, the British passed an Order in Council which was aimed at France but included all neutral countries as well. It stated that it would stop any ship on the high seas that it even suspected was headed for a Napoleonic port. At this time, this included most of the ports in Europe outside of England and a few northern countries. "By 1812 they had captured almost four hundred American vessels, some within sight of the U.S. coast, and played havoc with the American export trade."[4]

The Americans of course, could not tolerate this, what they considered to be high seas piracy, and more importantly could not long survive the economic depression that the blockade by the British enforced upon them. By the summer of 1812, three American armies were massed on the borders of Upper Canada, and it was feared if Ontario fell, then Quebec, or Lower Canada, would collapse soon after. On June 18, 1812, war was declared between England and the United States of America.

At sea, the Americans would need the help of the French to combat the powerful Royal Navy of Britain, while on land they hoped to invade the British colonies of Upper (Ontario) and Lower (Quebec) Canada, and make them a further extension of their United States. They planned to first take Upper Canada, or Ontario, since many of the settlers in the wild northwestern frontier were Americans themselves, having moved into the wild, unsettled country to escape the ever increasing population pressures from the east. But the hoped for support the Americans had counted on in the northwest

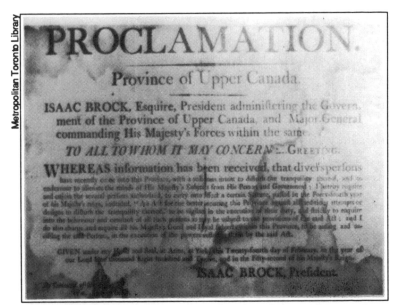

General Isaac Brock's Proclamation issued to the citizens of Upper Canada in 1812 was a call to arms for all loyal Canadians to resist the American invaders.

did not materialize when they began their invasion of Canada.

When the first shots were fired along the border in Upper Canada, British troops which had been gathering in Lower Canada, or Quebec, since 1807 were rushed to the farflung frontier to repulse the invaders. Among them were the men of the Royal Newfoundland Regiment who would see long and hard duty throughout the entirety of the war from 1812-1814.

The Newfoundlanders would see action on sea as well as on land, and many of them would be recognized for their seamanship and used to fight the large naval battles that were to come on the Great Lakes. The Regiment would also be used as everything from marines, sailors, navigators, gunners, shock troops, commandos — as well as in their conventional role — and finally as peacekeepers on the wild frontier in the aftermath of the war.[5]

General orders issued from headquarters in Quebec throughout the war constantly saw the elements of the Royal Newfoundland Regiment being ordered helter skelter to front lines or threatened positions in small, detached companies, into every service imaginable from ferrying troops in rowboats, to commanding warships on the Great Lakes. During the five years since its posting in Quebec in 1807, the Regiment had shown such great versatility in all aspects of military service that they had come to be regarded as the "Special Forces" of the Canadian Regiments.[6]

A year before the war officially began, their reputation as the "Boat Brigade" was already established. In anticipation of war, the British were dispersing troops from its headquarters in Quebec northwest along the Great Lakes to defend against an attack by the Americans against Upper Canada, Ontario. Late in 1811, a Canadian Regiment assigned to man far northern outposts along the shores of Lake Huron were to be transported there by; "A party of Newfoundlanders" who would "bring back the bateaux (boats) after landing the Regiment."[7]

Many of the Regular British Army troops, Canadian "army" soldiers and "mainland" militia who served with them soon came to affectionately call them the "Northerners." Contemporaries of the time and later observers commented; "...the 'Northerners' were men of iron, proof against cold weather, hard fare, and perils of all kinds," and that "they were a fine set of men, particularly the Company of Volunteer artillery selected from among the flower of the Inhabitants of St. John's." Others observed that, "their bravery, insensibility of fear, and contempt of danger is very remarkable...and nowhere can a stronger and more hardy race be found than in Newfoundland." Of their worth as sailors, a commander of the Royal Navy, (later defeated in a battle on the Great Lakes) told his superiors that one reason for his defeat was "the lack of good seamen arriving in time from Newfoundland; the authorities not aware of the urgent need of them."[8]

For their part, however, the Newfoundlanders seemed to remain a little aloof from their mainland comrades-in-arms. Perhaps it was due to the pride they felt in the part their Regiment played in the siege of Quebec in 1775 during the American Revolution. When marching alongside other regiments the Newfoundlanders would exclaim as they brushed alongside the others from milder climates; "I am a man of the 'north'," and then "eyed with contempt the men softened by the luxurious fare of bread and bacon."[9]

Despite their seeming cockiness, the "Northerners" and "Boat Brigade" were soon to prove that every moniker they had earned was well deserved. Because the Regiment was split up into so many detachments and would serve in so many different capacities, a General Order from headquarters in Quebec issued on June 30th, 1812 directed that "the colours of the Regiment (were) to be lodged in the Ordnance Armoury."[10]

Some of the Boat Brigade that had "ferried" the Canadian Regiment to the northern outposts of the great Lakes were themselves left to help garrison the forts. A handful of the Royal Newfoundland Regiment were left to complement Fort Joseph on an island of the same name at the head of Lake Huron, the last outpost of British presence in the wilderness frontier of the "northwest."

On July 15, 1812, Captain Charles Roberts, commanding the garrison, received word from General Isaac Brock, commander-in-chief of British forces in Upper Canada, that war had been declared and that he was to capture the American fort on Mackinac Island about 45 miles south of St. Joseph Island at the head of Lake Michigan.

Roberts had only forty-five regular army troops under his command and the handful of Newfoundlanders. He also had the armed brig *Caledonia*, and in the "Boat Brigade," the men who could sail her. Roberts, augmented his paltry force with 105 "voyageurs" and "courier de bois," and about 400 Indian allies of mixed tribes. With the "Boat Brigades" as his crew and navigators he sailed to Fort Mackinac early on the morning of July 16 followed by a flotilla of "bateaux" with their voyageurs and canoes with their Indians. He reached the island about midnight and by dawn had scaled its steep cliffs, hauling up one of the *Caledonia's* cannon with him.

While his Boat Brigade set up the gun on a point over-looking the fort, Roberts had his men go quietly through the town awakening the civilians and herding them to a place of safety. At dawn he fired a cannon shot over the fort, rousing the surprised garrison. He then entered the fort under a flag of truce, advising its commander, Lt. Hanks, that the fort was surrounded and demanded his surrender.

Lt. Hanks with only sixty men realized it would be suicide to resist. He surrendered the fort with its seven cannon and plentiful stores as well as 700 bundles of furs. The American gateway to the northwest of Upper Canada had been shut.[11]

Captain Roberts immediately sent word to Gen. Brock at Upper Canada headquarters in York (Toronto) of his success and Brock acted quickly at the news. He sent reinforcements to Roberts to hold Fort Mackinac, among them a detachment of twenty-five men of the Royal Newfoundland Regiment. They would help garrison and hold the fort throughout the war.

General Brock decided his next strategy. A large American force under command of General William Hull had arrived at Fort Detroit on the west side of the Detroit River across from the Canadian town of Sandwich. Hull had 2500 troops with him and was threatening to "liberate" Canada. Gen. Brock quickly raised a mixed force of 600 Indians, 400 militia, and 300 regular troops, among which was a detachment of fifty men of the Royal Newfoundland Regiment.

By August 5th, Brock was ready to sail across Lake Ontario and up Lake Erie to the Detroit River. He arrived at Fort Amherstburg just south of Sandwich on the evening of the thirteenth. After laying out his plans with his Indian allies — under the leadership of the famous Tecumseh — he moved his force to Sandwich on August 15th, directly across the river from Fort Detroit. After an invitation by Brock to Hull to surrender and a refusal by Hull to Brock, the two batteries opened cannon fire on each other across the Detroit River.

Tecumseh: Shawnee chief, he fought in several battles as an ally of the British, including the capture of Detroit with General Brock, and at Moraviantown on the Thames River where he was killed in 1813.

Late that night Tecumseh and his Indians in their canoes, and Brock and his troops in boats manned by a detachment of the Royal Newfoundland Regiment quietly crossed the river to the American side. At dawn on the morning of August 16th, Brock and Tecumseh marched on Fort Detroit as the British guns from Sandwich and the schooner *Queen Charlotte* bombarded the Americans. Caught by surprise and in complete confusion, Hull immediately surrendered the fort, virtually without firing a shot.[12]

General Hull, his officers and men were taken prisoner and embarked for Quebec. There, they would be exchanged for British prisoners of war. General Hull himself would be worth thirty British troops in exchange. To accomplish the transport, Gen. Brock again looked to the Royal Newfoundland Regiment. They would escort the prisoners and navigate the prison ships down the Great Lakes and the St. Lawrence River to Quebec City.

General Brock accompanied his prize and paraded the American prisoners through the streets of Montreal and Cornwall in a show of victory. On September 12, 1812 a Montreal newspaper reported that, "General Hull...accompanied by about twenty-five officers and 350 soldiers left Kingston under escort of 130 men commanded by Major Heathcote of the Newfoundland Regiment."[13]

Brock and the British had won their second bloodless victory of the young war, guaranteeing, at least initially, the security of their northwestern frontier. Of his bloodless victory, Gen. Brock had high praise for his men, and singled out the Newfoundland Regiment and their "Boat Brigade" who had sailed his armed schooner *Queen Charlotte* and manned his boats across the Detroit River, reported, "is deserving of every praise for their steadiness in the field as well as when embarked in the King's Vessels."[14]

General Brock's glowing praises of the Newfoundland Regiment at Fort Detroit earned three of the Newfoundland detachment, who were under the command of Captain Robert Mockley, the General Service Medal for their distinguished service in action.

Within a few days of his triumphant march into Quebec City, Gen. Brock was back at Kingston with his decorated heroes of the Royal Newfoundland Regiment. He was greeted with the news that the Americans were planning a strike from Fort Niagara across the river at Queenston on the Canadian side. He hurried to Fort George, just below Queenston, leaving orders for Captain Mockley and his Regiment to join him as soon as possible. On September 12th, the same day that the Montreal newspaper reported his passing through there a few days earlier, Brock wrote Governor Prevost at Quebec telling him that, "the 'Flank Companies' of the Royal Newfoundland Regiment have joined me."[15]

General Brock intended to use the Newfoundland Regiment's "Flanking Companies" as scouts and commandos to gather intelligence for him along the lower Niagara River concerning the planned American attack. On October 10th, he received a report from General Sheaffe at Fort Erie detailing the loss of two British warships and an urgent request for reinforcements. Gen. Sheaffe feared the Americans were planning a major attack on the upper Niagara River to coincide with one on the lower river.

Sheaffe reported that in the early morning hours of October 9th, the Americans had captured two British warships which had arrived the previous day and had anchored under the protection of the guns at Fort Erie. The two ships were armed brigs, the *Detroit* of six guns, captured by the British at Fort Detroit by Gen. Brock was a newly built American ship named the *Adam*, but was renamed the *Detroit* by the British, and the *Caledonia* of two guns, the same vessel used by the British in the capture of Fort Mackinac, owned by the North-West Fur Company, and "generously" seconded to the Royal Navy.

The two ships had lately arrived from Fort Detroit where they had spent the time since Brock's capture of the American post loading a cargo of captured muskets and ammunition, captured furs, and captured American soldiers. The ships were under the command of Lieutenant Frederick Rolette of the Royal Navy. His crew were all members of the Royal Newfoundland Regiment, along with a handful of "voyageurs" and "bateaux" men of the North-West Fur Company. The Newfoundlanders had been assigned the role of "marines" in escorting the ship and its cargo of prisoners and arms to Fort Erie.

The *Caledonia* was captained by a young Second-Lieutenant of the Royal Navy, Robert Irvine. He had with him only a dozen inexperienced sailing men of the North-West Company. In all the two crews numbered about forty men and they felt secure on the night of October 8th, anchored as they were under the protection of the guns of Fort Erie.

But about three o'clock on the morning of October 9th, two American gunboats containing fifty men each rowed towards the two ships under cover of a driving rain and sleet storm. Each of the American boats headed towards one of the British ships.

The Americans targeted the *Detroit* first, she being one of their own ships and the more valuable of the two with her six guns and cargo of arms and prisoners. The Americans succeeded in cutting the mooring and setting the ship adrift, and were boarding before they were discovered.

A surprised sentry gave the, "All hands on deck!" call but by then it was too late. Lt. Rolette and his second in command, Ensign Thomas Kerr rushed out from their cabins and engaged the boarders in battle along with the other marines on duty on deck. They were greatly out-numbered and although they put up a stiff resistance they were soon overpowered, Ensign Kerr and nine of the other marines being wounded.

The other marines below decks who scurried to get above

decks upon hearing the alarm were hampered in the passage and stairways by the "voyageurs" who were retreating below decks. Sergeant William Woodlands upon rushing on the deck was "struck by a cutlass and thrown down the hatchway." Another soldier, Private Louis Fervet, after hearing the call for "all hands on deck" rushed to the arms chest where he was "seized by some man and knocked down the hatchway."[16]

By now the *Caledonia* had also been boarded but her captain resisted with gunfire before the ship's crew were overpowered. Alerted by the gunfire, the batteries atop the river at Fort Erie spotted the two ships drifting across the river towards the American side. They immediately opened fire on the two ships, which, without hoisted sails were like the proverbial sitting ducks.

Both ships went aground, the *Caledonia* — luckily, on the American shore of the river just below the protective gun battery at Black Rocks. The *Detroit*, however, went aground on an island, called Squaw Island, in the mouth of the river and, unfortunately for the Americans, on the Canadian side of the island. The guns of Fort Erie continued to pound the *Detroit* throughout the early morning by which time its sails were in tatters.

Under the constant bombardment of the British guns, the Americans were forced to abandon the beached ship taking its crew ashore as prisoners of war. The British were not so eager to abandon the *Detroit*. Later that day they sent a strong force in boats to Squaw Island where they tried desperately to free the ship and return it to the Canadian side of the river.

The Americans launched a strong counter-attack and drove the British back but not before they had dumped the six cannon overboard. They managed to salvage some of the ship's cargo of arms and ammunition and succeeded in

raising the six cannon. With the Americans again in possession of the ship, the guns from Fort Erie again began to
bombard the ship. Realizing they could not refloat the vessel
they decided to scuttle her and left her in flames on the beach
of Squaw Island.[17]

In response to Gen. Sheaffe's report and request for
reinforcement, Gen. Brock sent his just arrived "Flanking
Companies" of the Royal Newfoundland Regiment up the
thirty mile stretch of the Niagara River to Fort Erie. Commanding the Newfoundlanders was Captain Whelan, whose
small force of "commandos" was placed under the orders of
Major Ormsby who also had contingents of the 41st and 49th
Regiments under his command at the fort.

The day of Capt. Whelan's departure for Fort Erie, October 13, 1812, the Americans launched a full scale attack across
the Niagara River against Queenston Heights. They were
eventually beaten back across the river after a severe battle
which saw very high casualties on both sides, among them
General Brock himself who was shot and killed by an American sniper.[18]

PROFILE; THE BATTLE OF QUEENSTON HEIGHTS

General (Sir) Isaac Brock
1769-1812

The Battle of Queenston Heights on October 13, 1812 was the first real American offensive of the War of 1812-1814. It was undertaken almost desperately after being handed two stunning defeats at Mackinac Island and Fort Detroit by the fiery British commander General Sir Isaac Brock. By October 10th, the American Commander on the Niagara River, General Solomon Van Rensselaer, had amassed 6,300 troops on the American side of the river opposite the small town of Queenston. Once again, the American adversary would be the intrepid Brock.[19]

Brock, expecting an attack had concentrated his force at Fort George at the mouth of the river on Lake Ontario. He had also reinforced strategic points along the river and had sent 350 men with three field guns to garrison Queenston. Van Rensselaer had gone to great pains to bluff Brock as to where his point of attack would be, and it worked. On October 10th, the American attempted their invasion at Queenston. Bad weather and strong currents forced the Americans to abandon their crossing and when the attempt was reported to Brock he brushed it off as a feint intended to draw him away with his main force from the real target, Fort George.

Van Rensselaer's strategy was working. Brock did not

Public Archives of Canada

Major-General Stephan Van Rensselaer commanded the American troops at the Battle of Queenston Heights, and was later forced to resign in disgrace due to his "embarrassing" defeat.

Van Rensselaer's strategy was working. Brock did not respond to his attempted landing. So in early morning on October 13th, the Americans launched their attack in earnest. Van Rensselaer himself led the assault, leading 225 of his men up the steep bluffs to the top of Queenston Heights. He was met by a stiff resistance from the garrison which had among it elements of the Royal Newfoundland Regiment. The Americans were driven back down the cliffs but were able to continue landing infantry on the beach below.

A few miles downriver of Fort George the booming of the cannon at Queenston Heights, alerted General Brock that he may have been wrong in his assumption. He had been suffering with some slight illness for the past few days but he immediately jumped up from his bed, hurriedly dressed, mounted his horse and galloped off for Queenston, leaving orders with his second-in-command, General Sheaffe to march with all troops as soon as possible. As he rode onto the crest of Queenston Heights he found that his garrison still had the Americans pinned down below, but boats were landing more and more bluecoats by the minute.

Now, Brock made the first — and what turned out to be the last — tactical error of his military career. He ordered Captain Williams, commanding the garrison, to go down to the river flats around Queenston and attempt to stop the handful of men atop the heights with himself to continue firing the cannons on the Americans below. Brock believed the heights to be impregnable once the crest was under control.

What he didn't know was that the heights were accessible from behind by a long winding path up from the river through thick shrubs and trees. Van Rensselaer found an American smuggler among his ranks and sent him to guide Captain Wool and two hundred men up the winding, hidden trail. Brock and his handful of defenders knew nothing until the Americans rushed out of the woods behind them. Brock himself was nearly captured as he and his men scrambled to escape down the slopes to the village of Queenston below.

Here, Brock compounded his error. His cannons were now in the hands of the Americans and being used against him. Thinking the American company that had surprised his flank was only a small one, he decided to rush up the hill and recapture the cannon and the crest before reinforcements arrived. He took Captain Williams and 100 men of the 49th Regiment and charged up the slopes. Brock in the lead, waving his sword and urging his men on. For a moment the Americans began to retreat to the crest of the heights, but Captain Wool rallied his troops and they counterattacked forcing the British back down the slopes. General Brock stood his ground. Some of the men in the attack were from his own 49th Regiment and he yelled after them, "This is the first time I have ever seen the 49th turn their backs!"[20]

Rallied once more, the redcoats once again rushed up the slopes, still led by their valiant General. A sharpshooting American rifleman spotted Brock as their leader and with one well placed shot from about thirty paces dropped him with a bullet in his heart. Broken by the death of their leader, most of the British retreated down the slopes with Brock's body and sought cover in the village of Queenston. Some of the 49th Regiment, however, under Captain Williams found cover in some woods about halfway up the slopes.

Below, in Queenston, Major MacDonell, one of Brock's aides, was reinforced by two companies of militia. MacDonell decided to follow the lead of his slain commander. He stormed back up the slopes and managed to reach the woods where Captain Williams and the remnants of his 49th were held up. Together, the two officers prepared a plan for an all out assault on the crest of the heights.

Their efforts were no more successful than their leader's. American sharpshooters shot down man after man as they struggled up the exposed slopes. Among them were both Williams and MacDonell, both singled out because of their rank and both shot down; Williams seriously wounded and MacDonell mortally. The redcoats retreated once again to the cover of the woods on the slopes and waited for some officer to take charge of their situation.

Captain Dennis, who had been defending the river flats at Queenston village, hurried up to the shaky British position and made probably the most sensible decision of the battle. He organized the troops into an orderly retreat back down the slopes to Queenston.

By the time he arrived there, so too had General Sheaffe with the 41st Regiment from Fort George. He agreed with Captain Dennis' decision that another assault up the slopes would be suicide as hundreds of Americans were now swarming up the bluffs of the heights and crowding the hilltop. Sheaffe decided to take the 41st Regiment, a couple of militia companies and about fifty Indian allies that had joined him on his way from Fort George, and outflanked the Americans from the same spot they had outflanked Brock.

General Sheaffe worked his way slowly and quietly in a

wide circle around and through the woods into a position to attack the American flank. He then sent the Indians thrashing through the woods shrilling their chilling warwhoops and sounding like they were hundreds instead of dozens. The startled Americans, many of them militiamen who were in great fear of the Indians, began to panic. When Sheaffe's orderly column of redcoats burst from the trees, many of the bluecoats were already retreating towards the crest of the bluffs.

One American officer attempted to rally his men but by now many of them were scurrying down the steep bluffs to the boats below. Captain Dennis and his redcoats rushed up the slopes from Queenston and within minutes the American force was surrounded. There was a long standoff as the forces faced each other. During the standoff, the American commander, Brigadier Wadsworth, who by now had landed a force equal to that of the British, learned that 1,700 militiamen which he had counted on as reinforcements, refused to cross the river to join the battle. The boats would not even cross the river to pick up the American troops stranded on the beach below the bluffs. Without reinforcements, and more importantly, without a resupply of powder and shot, Wadsworth realized it would be suicide to resist. He reluctantly waved the white flag.

The British took over 900 American prisoners, among them seventy-five officers. American dead were over 200. British casualties had been miraculously light. They had lost only 14 killed and about 80 wounded, most of them in the brave but foolhardy attacks by Brock and MacDonell.[21]

For the British, the Battle of Queenston Heights was their most glorious victory of the war. But, it was also their most tragic loss. Nobody believed that their most brilliant and courageous General, Sir Isaac Brock could be replaced.[22]

Endnotes:

1. Webber; op. cit., p. 533.

2. O'Flaherty; op. cit., p. 351.

3. O'Neill; *The Oldest City*, p. 103.

4. Berton, Pierre; *The Invasion of Canada 1812-1813.* p. 25.

5. O'Flaherty; op. cit., p. 551.

6. Saunders, Dr. Robert; "When Newfoundland Helped Save Canada", *New-foundland Quarterly*, Vol. 50, No. 33, 1950, p. 10. During its years of service in the War of 1812-14, the Royal Newfoundland Regiment earned several "nicknames," among them the "Northmen," the "Boat Brigade," the "Sleigh Establishment" owing to their equipping themselves with snowshoes and "creeper" for winter campaigns, and the "Mississippi Volunteers."

7. Ibid.

8. Ibid.

9. Ibid.

10. Ibid. Detached, and serving under the colours of other Regiments as they were, the Newfoundlanders may have felt the need to prove themselves as good a fighting force as any other, and this may have contributed to their cockiness.

11. Sylvestor, William; "Michilimackinac: The Bloodless War." *Canadian Frontier.* 1976, p. 73.

12. Raddal; op. cit., p. 201.

13. Saunders; op. cit., p. 23.

14. Ibid.

15. Ibid. The "Flanking Companies" of the Royal Newfoundland Regiment, as General Brock designated them, were in what today's military terms would be called "commandoes," special squads of men sent behind enemy lines to "outflank" and disrupt their front lines of attack.

16. Saunders; op. cit., p. 36.

17. Berton; op. cit., p. 227.

18. Raddal; op. cit., p. 206. Brock's coat is preserved in the National Archives of Canada, a "memento to a very gallant gentleman, and a tribute to American marksmanship."

19. Raddal; op. cit., p. 204.

20. Berton; op. cit., p. 240.

21. Raddal; op. cit., p. 207.

22. Whalen, Dwight; "The Restless Tombs of Isaac Brock." *Canadian Frontier.* Vol. 3, No. 2, 1974. (Garnet Publishing Co., Langley, B.C., p. 11-13). Brock was knighted posthumously for his valour at Queenston Heights. In death, he seemed to incur as much excitement and controversy as he did in life. After his death he was given a state funeral and buried at Fort George. Twelve years later it was decided to build a monument to the memory of the "hero of Canada" on the site of his death. A 130 foot high monument was begun construction on that year and Brock's remains were exhumed and reburied under it. Along with Brock's remains, the later infamous "rebel" William Lyon MacKenzie buried one of his "rebel" newspapers in the tomb so it was demolished halfway through its construction, then built up again — purged of the "rebel trash" of MacKenzie. In 1840, another "spurned" rebel, Benjamin Lett blew up Brock's monument. The memorial and grave of Brock stood in ruins for twelve years, until work got underway to rebuild it in 1852. While the

work was being done, Brock's remains were moved to a private cemetery in the town of Queenston. In 1856 the new monument, reaching 190 feet into the skyline was completed and Brock's remains were again moved to his latest resting place. It was Brock's fourth "state funeral" in almost 150 years. Today, Brock's monument and his remains still rest on Queenston Heights, perhaps, finally in peace.

CHAPTER SIX

Attack on the American Frontier

OLLOWING THE BATTLE OF QUEENSTON HEIGHTS the Americans and British agreed on a three day amnesty — to care for the wounded, bury the dead and exchange prisoners — some 1,000 of whom had been taken by the British alone. The British held General Hull whom the Americans were anxious to repatriate and the British wanted Lt. Rolette and his Newfoundlanders back, although it seems they wanted Rolette back for different reasons than the Americans wanted Hull returned.

The British also took steps to reinforce Fort Erie, which they recognized after the Lt. Rolette — "Detroit" affair was dangerously undermanned. At this time there was only a company and a half of Newfoundlanders at the Fort, 126 men, under the command of Major Ormsby. In response for the request for reinforcements, Lt. Governor George Prevost in Quebec City wrote London: "I have now to state the difficulties which attend providing them (Fort Erie) with proper officers and suitable crews. For the present I have allotted the Newfoundland Fencibles for that service."[1] These orders were issued for the Regiment's Companies headquartered at Kingston but there was a delay of a week or so as the Regiment prepared.

Royal Ontario Museum

Kingston: Headquarters of the Royal Newfoundland Regiment during the war of 1812-1814.

A prisoner exchange had been arranged and Prevost wanted the Regiment up to its full complement before it marched. "The light company of the Newfoundland Regiment," his orders read, "will hold itself in immediate readiness to march for Fort Erie. These men belonging to the Newfoundland Regiment and lately returned from being prisoners of war will be equipped with arms and be furnished with clothing, so as to be able to march with the light company of the Regiment."[2]

While Fort Erie waited for its reinforcements, Lt. Rolette and the Newfoundland "marines" captured on the "Detroit" had also been returned in a prisoner exchange. A Court of Inquiry was set up at Fort Erie to see if there was any blame to be placed for the loss of the captured American vessel. On October 27th, Major General Shaw commenced the Inquiry, taking the testimony of Lt. Rolette and the Newfoundland Regiment "marines" captured with him.

Lt. Rolette testified, "At 7 P.M. the watch was set consisting of six men with arms and at three o'clock A.M. one of the watch came down into the cabin and said that he saw a boat going onboard the *Caledonia* ... on my coming up on deck with Ensign Kerr of the Newfoundland Fencibles, I perceived the *Detroit* adrift and a boat alongside ... also another boat with two officers and thirty soldiers of the U.S. Army.

"Being asked to surrender, I refused, on which the soldiers immediately commenced a fire of musketry ... I resisted and defended the vessel with nine men and Ensign Kerr wounded ...the remainder being knocked down the hatchway, the enemy got possession of the vessel."[3]

On several of the "marines" being called, they all supported their commander's story, saying that they were surprised in the foggy and stormy night and being greatly outnumbered were soon overwhelmed and taken prisoner. Lt. Rolette and his crew of Newfoundlanders were cleared of any dereliction of duty and the matter was dropped.

In early November, the Companies of the Royal Newfoundland Regiment sent to reinforce the fort, arrived at Erie under the command of Captain Whelan, swelling the fort's numbers to almost 500 men. Some of them were detached into smaller companies and sent to man strategic points along the seventeen mile stretch of the Upper Niagara River from the fort to the falls.

During the amnesty declared after the Battle of Queenston Heights, the British used the time to reclaim their prisoners of war and to reinforce Fort Erie. But they were only thinking defence. The Americans were planning offence. General Van Rensselaer had been forced to resign in disgrace after the fiasco at Queenston Heights, and a regular Army officer, General Smyth took control of the American forces on the Niagara River. While the British consolidated its defences, Smyth was readying his offences.[4]

Gen. Smyth's plan was to abandon attempts to capture the lower Niagara and force his way into Lake Ontario, and instead to capture Fort Erie, control the upper Niagara, and thus the gateway to Lake Erie and the upper Great Lakes beyond. He spent the month of November gathering troops and building boats for his strike across the Niagara.

By late November, Smyth had moved 4,500 troops from the lower Niagara to a place called Black Rock on the upper Niagara across from Fort Erie at the head of the river. From here, he planned to launch his invasion of "Upper Canada." His strategy was to isolate Fort Erie from any help down-river, then capture it at his leisure. To do this he planned to take a small British garrison at a place called Frenchman's Creek about five miles downriver from the fort and about ten miles upriver from the British headquarters on the upper Niagara, Chippewa.

Smyth reasoned that if he could destroy the battery of three cannon and the bridge over Frenchman's Creek, he could cut communications and transportation between the two British strongholds on the river. He would then hold the strategic point isolating Fort Erie which he could surround, beseige and finally capture. The plan was sound and might have succeeded had not the Americans blundered once again.

At Chippewa, the British commander, Colonel Cecil Bis-shopp had only 1,000 men under his command including regulars and Canadian militia. He too, like Commander Shaw at Fort Erie had spread his men in small garrisons along the ten mile stretch of the river from Chippewa to French-man's Creek.

British spies had reported Smyth's movements and the large number of troops he was amassing near Black Rock. Col. Bisshopp was sure he was planning a full scale attack either on Fort Erie or Chippewa. His reports to General Sheaffe at Fort George, now commanding all British forces in Upper Canada, led the Commander-in-chief to debate abandoning Fort Erie altogether and concentrating his troops at Chippewa at the top of Niagara Falls.

Colonel Bisshopp and senior officers argued hotly with him against this strategy, pointing out that if Fort Erie was lost the Americans would control the upper Great Lakes and easily capture Fort Detroit and Fort Mackinac which were footholds in the northwest. While Sheaffe vacillated the men at Fort Erie waited in uncertainty. One of the fort's officers later recorded: "Had the enemy gained possession of Fort Erie at this period it would have been impossible to dislodge them. Our duty was exceedingly severe, cold weather, and lying on our arms every night, being in constant expectation of attack."[5]

On the night of November 27th, Gen. Smyth made his move to capture Fort Erie. He loaded his boats with 400 troops and sent them across the river in a four or five mile front from Fort Erie to Frenchman's Creek, hoping the small sporadic attacks all along the river would keep the British confused and prevent them from concentrating their forces at Frenchman's Creek.

The diversionary attacks took place in thick woods on a windy night with thick squalls of sleet and snow. The weather and the widespread skirmishes created a great deal of confusion, which saw both sides often firing on friend and foe alike.

Smyth's main attack force succeeded in reaching the British battery at Frenchman's Creek and drove the redcoats from the position. The Americans captured the three guns and trained them on the road from Chippewa. The second groups of attackers sent to take out the bridge over Frenchman's Creek proved to be Smyth's undoing. The Americans fought their way to the bridge and took possession of it but once in control discovered that the axes they had brought with them with which to cut the bridge down had been left in the boats at the river.[6]

By now Fort Erie had been alerted by the cannon fire of the guns at Frenchman's Creek and the sporadic firefights in the woods along the road. Major Ormsby was ordered to take the 49th Regiment and some of the Newfoundland "Flanking Company" and rush to the aid of the battery at Frenchman's Creek. Captain Whelan and the bulk of the Royal Newfoundland Regiment were left at Fort Erie to defend the post at all costs. The Americans, by now confused and hesitant were pinned down by Ormsby and his men and had no way of completing their mission. Minutes later Col. Bisshopp arrived on the scene with 200 Canadian militia from Chippewa and catching the bluecoats in a pincer action, the Americans were forced to withdraw from the battery and the bridge, scrambling back across the river leaving several dead and thirty-eight prisoners in British hands.

Bisshopp remounted the cannon in the battery and leaving some of the militia to reinforce it went on the Fort Erie with Ormsby where he took temporary command of the post. There was no doubt now as to what Smyth's object of attack was to be. He was after Fort Erie.

With daylight of November 28th, the American guns at Black Rock opened up a heavy bombardment on the British fort. The fury and thunderous pounding of the cannonade prompted one American observer to comment, "Lieut. Stevens poured his cannon balls into Fort Erie so well that the enemy hoisted a white flag," but since the fort did not surrender, he added, "whether as a sign of surrender or not we cannot say."[7] For all its fury, the American bombardment had little effect on the Fort or its defenders.

The next morning the troops of Fort Erie watched almost in awe as thousands of American troops boarded boats in what looked to the British to be an attempted, all-out daylight assault on the guns of Fort Erie. The Americans milled about the shoreline below Black Rock for most of the day but made no attempt to cross. Late that afternoon Smyth sent a boat across the river with a flag of truce.

Smyth demanded the immediate surrender of the Fort, in order to, as he put it, avoid "useless effusion of blood." Col. Bisshopp returned him a very polite message saying that he "should have the honour of taking it (Fort Erie) by force of arms, not by negotiating."[8]

While Smyth waited for Bisshopp's reply, the more prudent of his officers had been trying to convince him of the folly of a headlong daylight attack on the fort. When he received Bisshopp's polite refusal, he acquiesced to the advice of his junior officers. As dusk came on he went down to the shoreline to tell his men, many of whom had been sitting in the cramped boats all day in freezing temperatures and falling snow, that they were to, "Disembark and dine!"[9] The invasion was off for today.

Two days later on December 1st, Smyth attempted another "invasion." That evening he began loading his boats for another crossing. It took all night to organize the embarkation and by dawn of the next day Smyth found himself with another problem — mutinous militia. A regiment of Pennsylvania volunteers refused to board the boats and cross the river. They claimed that they had joined up to protect the borders of the United States, not invade a foreign country. Soon other companies of volunteers and militia joined them. It was the same scenario as Queenston Heights, one which probably cost the Americans a victory there. Smyth knew that he could not capture Fort Erie without the support of the militia and volunteers so he threw up his hands and declared that the war on the Niagara River for 1812 was over. Cancelled because of winter.[10]

Fort Erie and Upper Canada were secure and the men of the Royal Newfoundland Regiment settled in for a long and isolated winter.

Not all of the Royal Newfoundland Regiment at Fort Erie settled in there for the winter. Lt. Frederick Rolette, his Second Lt. Robert Irvine, along with Ensign Kerr and his small company of Newfoundland "Marines" were returned to their home posting at Fort Amherstburg on the Detroit River. If war had been cancelled on the Niagara frontier because of winter, it had not been cancelled on the northwestern frontier at Lake Erie.

Fort Amherstburg, since the capture of Fort Detroit the previous year, had become the British headquarters of operation in the northwest. It was the main supply base for the captured Fort Detroit, as well as the British posts at Mackinac and St. Joseph's Island in the far northern reaches of Lake Huron. As the winter of 1812-13 settled in, the British forces at Fort Amherstburg were also content to settle in and simply guard their borders. They were not the aggressors on this border war and had no intention of carrying the fight to the invaders without being properly prepared. The Americans, however, were pressing their plans to take over Upper Canada.

All that winter their armies were marching in the west towards Lake Erie and the British stronghold at Amherstburg and their own captured fort at Detroit. On January 11, 1813 General James Winchester of the regular American Army arrived at the Maumee River on the southern shore of Lake Erie about sixty miles from Fort Amherstburg with an army of 1,000 troops, most of them enthusiastic, patriotic Kentucky volunteers.

Winchester had orders to construct a hurried camp of huts and appear to be setting in for the winter. The ruse was an attempt to make the British think that he was preparing for a spring strike up the Detroit River to recapture their lost fort. Winchester's actual orders were to wait for the deep winter freeze then swiftly strike out across the lake with his entire force and attack and capture Fort Amherstburg.[11]

Two days later, Lt. Col. Henry Procter, senior British officer on the Detroit frontier and commanding at Fort Amherstburg, learned of the American presence on the Maumee River from his Indian scouts. Procter believed exactly what Winchester wanted him to, that the Americans were planning a spring attack on Fort Detroit. Knowing the advance force of Americans were isolated, Procter decided to block their advance by destroying any possible source of supplies on their route.

On the American side of the Detroit River, almost twenty-six miles below Fort Amherstburg, was a small town populated mostly by French-Canadians, appropriately named Frenchtown. It was built on both banks of a small creek called the Raisin River which flowed into the Detroit River. The town, Procter knew, would be well supplied with winter stores of flour, grains and other provisions which the Americans would need to resupply themselves on their march to Fort Detroit.

The Canadian commander decided to capture Frenchtown, seize its supplies, destroy the town, and remove its inhabitants to the Canadian side of the river to keep them from rendering any aid to the Americans. On January 14, he sent a company of militia and two flanking companies of the Royal Newfoundland Regiment across the Detroit River to carry out his plan.[12]

The people of Frenchtown, of course, did not want to be moved. They resented and resisted the British highhandedness and some of them appealing to Winchester to come to their aid, offering him a bribe of "three thousand barrels of flour and much grain." Winchester needed the provisions and the help of the locals, so on January 18, he sent 450 regular army troops and Kentucky riflemen to take Frenchtown from the British.

The Americans attacked the town about 3 o'clock in the afternoon and although outnumbering the small British force, the redcoats fought ferociously for almost two hours, when by dusk they had been driven into the woods on the north side of the Raisin River. With news of the victory, Winchester rushed to bring up his remaining 500 troops and consolidated his bountiful prize. He felt that with the provisions and comforts that Frenchtown afforded he could launch his attacks on both Fort Amherstburg and Fort Detroit with success. Confident, the Americans settled into the town for a comfortable stay until spring. But while the bluecoats rested, the redcoats were on the move.[13]

At Fort Amherstburg, Lt. Col. Procter was preparing an immediate counter-attack. On the evening of January 19th, the day after the battle at Frenchtown he had his entire garrison of about 1,000 men made up of regular troops and militia and about 500 Indians, marching across the frozen Lake Erie towards the American position.

In the vanguard of the march was a detachment of the Royal Newfoundland Regiment, the "Sleigh Establishment" as they were called because they had equipped themselves with snowshoes and "creepers" —the sleds or "catamarans," which were used extensively in Newfoundland for winter travel. In this campaign, the "Sleigh Establishment" was made up of a company of Newfoundland "marines" who had been engaged in the battle for the ships *Caledonia* and *Detroit* at Fort Erie the previous fall. Once again they were led by their courageous officers, Lt. Frederick Rolette, and Second Lt. Irvine and Ensign Kerr.

The job of the "Sleigh Establishment" was to press ahead of the main column, dragging the field guns — three, 3-pounder cannons and three slightly lighter howitzers — across the ice on their sleds.[14]

Two hours before dawn on the bitterly cold morning of the 21st, Procter's troops and Indians were nearly ready to strike. The American sentries had either retreated inside out of the cold, or were asleep as were the rest of the troops. Procter's Indians led the redcoats into positions around the town until it was completely surrounded.

Procter however, hesitated and made a mistake that was to cost many of his soldiers their lives needlessly. His light companies of infantry and live-off-the-land Indians had been able to move into position before the heavily-laden detachment of "Sleigh Establishment" Newfoundlanders with their cannon cargoes could. Procter refused to press his advantage of surprise until his artillery was in position. His decision was to cost him dearly.

Not all the American sentries were asleep. One of them, a sharpshooting Kentuckian, spotted an advance patrol of the British and shot its leader through the head. The time for surprise had passed. Procter's Indians burst from their concealment and swarmed the town howling their war cries. The British troops followed, advancing in their orderly fashion.

By now, Lt. Rolette and his "Sleigh Establishment" of Newfoundlanders had joined the main force. Procter placed them at the centre of his attack, situating one of the guns directly in front of his advance. The gunners were not only being fired upon by the Americans but were also in danger of being shot from behind by their own men!

As the American defenders began to concentrate their fire on the British advance, the gunners at Procter's centre were forced to abandon their cannon, being caught in a savage crossfire between friend and foe alike. Seeing the gun abandoned, some of the Americans jumped over their palisades in an attempt to capture the cannon. Lt. Rolette, manning one of the flank guns, rallied his company of Newfoundlanders and rushed to rescue the artillery piece. A musket ball hit Rolette in the head and he dropped as if dead. As some of his men scrambled off the field with his body, Second Lt. Irvine pressed on with a handful of the "Sleigh Establishment" and reached the gun before the Americans. Grabbing the cannon rope, Irvine and his Newfoundlanders, under heavy fire, managed to drag the piece back to the British lines.[15]

By now the British Infantry and Indians had penetrated into the very centre of Frenchtown. Pockets of the Americans put up a valiant but futile fight, but most were caught sleeping and quickly taken captive, among them General Winchester who was taken in his nightshirt. Those who tried to fight back were shot down or tomahawked by the Indians. Those who were not captured, fled in disarray across the Raisin River where they were hotly pursued by the Indians into the woods, hunted down, and slaughtered.[16]

Frenchtown, like Detroit before it, now became the second British foothold on American soil. But it had been a costly victory for Procter. His hesitancy had cost him 182 casualties among his regular troops, and his unbridled tolerance of the Indian's savagery towards the American prisoners was to account for an even greater loss in the months to come.

On the Maumee River, General William Henry Harrison — Gen. Winchester's support commander — halted his advance down the river when he learned of the defeat and massacre at Frenchtown. Although he had 1,300 troops with him, the reports of the Indians' massacre of his men struck terror into his heart. He incorrectly believed that the British force at Amherstburg was larger than he had thought and he was now without almost half his force. Harrison hurriedly threw up a rough fort of thick logs and earthen works enclosing an area of eight acres just below the falls on the Maumee River and named the site Fort Meigs.

Procter soon learned that Harrison had halted his advance and was digging in to await reinforcements in the spring. He used the long, cold winter months to prepare a plan of attack before Harrison's help arrived.

Sir George Prevost, Governor-General of Canada and supreme commander of British forces in the War of 1812.

While war took a respite on the Niagara and Northwestern fronts, it did not cease on the most eastern frontier. On February 6, 1813 an American force crossed the frozen St. Lawrence River and attacked the small village of Elizabethtown near Prescott. They took several of the townspeople and a great store of provisions of the town and returned to their fort at Ogdensburg across the St. Lawrence. At Prescott, Colonel MacDonell of the Glengarry Regiment decided to exercise the option given to him by Governor Prevost to deal with the troublesome

American outpost which had long been a torment to the British all along the St. Lawrence River from Montreal to Kingston.

During the two weeks following the American attack on Elizabethtown, MacDonell planned his attack on Fort Ogdensburg. His force was undermanned and he suffered from a lack of officers to lead his troops. Besides his own Regiment of Glengarries, he had a company of Canadian Militia. The Militia and Artillery at his disposal had no officers in their ranks so MacDonell detached Colonel Fraser and Lieutenant Le Lievre of the Newfoundland Regiment to command them.

The companies of the Royal Newfoundland Regiment were left in charge of their non-commissioned officers.[17] MacDonell crossed the frozen St. Lawrence on February 22nd, with two columns of troops and an advance guard, once again made up of the Sleigh Establishment of the Royal Newfoundland Regiment. To the left of MacDonell's column of Glengarries was the second column of the 8th Regiment of Foot complemented by a small company of Newfoundlanders who were to act as artillery men under the command of Col. Fraser. Bringing up the rear was the Canadian Militia under the command of Lt. Le Lievre.

The snow drifts were deep and the going very tough but the trail was broken by the snowshoe-plodding Newfoundlanders of the Sleigh Establishment. MacDonell surprised the town of Ogdensburg where many of the American troops were idling out the winter. The advance guard of Newfoundlanders soon had them routed and on the run. Some of them reached the temporary safety of the fort but most were scattered into the woods beyond.

With the town secured, MacDonell used his time to rest his men and bring up his artillery. He also called on the fort to surrender but the American commander refused, answer-

Signal Hill Tattoo. Photos: B. Fardy

In battle, individual companies of British troops would spread out abreast in two files to face the enemy. Both files would "genuflect" to load their muskets (above), then the rear file would rise as the front file remained kneeling (below). At the centre of the company the "colour" party and the drummers would form up to have the troops "rally 'round the flag."

ing his request with cannonfire. Once his own guns were in place, MacDonell bombarded the fort and "silenced the enemy's battery fire." With the American guns out of action, the

British commander decided to storm the walls with fixed bayonets. In one terrific onslaught, led by the Newfoundland advance guard, his troops scaled the walls and quickly captured its greatly outnumbered garrison.

Although suffering considerable losses himself, Mac-Donell carried the day and won a considerable prize for the British. The American force was scattered and in retreat, most of it not stopping until it was nine miles from Ogdensburg. At the fort, the British took seventy prisoners and captured eleven guns, several hundred stacks of muskets, and a great quantity of military stores and provisions. Mac-Donell then burned the fort as well as two armed schooners and several gunboats and transport vessels which were frozen helpless in the ice. With the fort destroyed, his prisoners and booty in tow, MacDonell returned to his base in Prescott. The thorn in the Canadian side of the St. Lawrence River that had been Fort Ogdensburg had been deftly, and definitely removed.

Of the part the Royal Newfoundland Regiment played in the destruction of Fort Ogdensburg, Col. MacDonell wrote Deputy Adjutant General Harvey at Quebec City on February 25th, "I am much indebted to Captain Le Lievre for his active superintendence of the Militia to which I had attached him...(and) I must not forget to mention the brave conduct of the Newfoundland Company who had no officer of the regiment with them and led the advance guard."[18]

Now, as the cold claws of winter's month of March gripped the entire country, war did cease on all fronts along the Canadian-American border. But spring would come early and with it a more furious and fervent warfare.

PROFILE: GENERAL (SIR) ISAAC BROCK —
"HERO OF CANADA"

The name Isaac Brock immediately brings to the minds of Canadians the Battle of Queenston Heights, and the hero of the War of 1812-1814 who saved Canada from the expansionist and warmongering aspirations of the Americans south of the border. The name conjures up a romantic vision of the gallant commander mounted on his big chestnut stallion, Alfred, galloping past the farms along the Niagara River at sunrise, resplendent in his bright scarlet tunic and tall cocked hat, his waist girded by a gaudy Shawnee Indian sash, his black coat flying in the wind behind the sure, steeled hooves of his faithful mount, shouting to all that could hear him "The Americans are coming!"[19]

Truly a romantic and endearing image, and despite its seeming histrionics, basically a true one. Isaac Brock was a soldier. What he did for Canada he did out of a sense of duty, not out of any love for the fledgling country to which he had been, in his own mind, "sentenced" to serve. In reality, he disliked Canada, distrusted its people when it came to warfare, and longed to be somewhere else where he could better serve his king and country. But as a soldier, he was dedicated to doing his duty, no matter what, or where, that duty might be.

Brock was born at St. Peter Port, Guernsey, on October 6, 1769 and joined the British army at an early age. He advanced gradually through the ranks, earning his advancement on the field of battle. He was with the Duke of York as a young officer when the Duke engaged the French during the Napoleonic Wars at Egmont-OP-Zee in Holland on October 2, 1799.[20] The young officer caught the attention of the Duke, and Brock was given command of the 49th (Irish) Regiment of Foot, which in the Duke's opinion was one of the worst in the service, and which Brock turned into one of the best. Brock was a Lt-Colonel in charge of his rejuvenated 49th Regiment in April of 1801 when he was assigned duty aboard Admiral Nelson's fleet which sailed against the Danes at Copenhagen, and broke their resolve to resist the British blockade of northern Europe.[21]

In 1802 Brock was stationed in the Caribbean where he earned a reputation for brashness, courage, and leadership. He showed he was a man of action, not merely words. On one occasion, accepting a dare, he rode his horse to the top of a precipitous hill which everyone considered could not be done. On another, he was challenged to a duel by a particular braggart who was particularly good with a pistol at twelve paces. Brock accepted his challenge, but as the challenged set his own terms. He would confront the duellist at one pace, virtually face-to-face. the duelling braggart retracted his challenge and was forced to resign from the regiment.[22]

Brock was posted to Canada in 1803 and had no sooner arrived when his superiors learned first-hand of the reputation which had preceded him. When six of his regiment deserted, Brock personally led an eight-hour chase in an open boat across Lake Ontario to apprehend them. He was reprimanded for his action but his high command recognised at once the mettle of the man with whom they would be dealing.[23]

By 1807, Brock was warning his superiors of the gathering war clouds below the border. If his superiors were in agreement they were not ready to admit he was right. It appears they simply hoped he was wrong, and wished the gathering clouds would dissipate. The wily and impetuous Lt.-Colonel however, was determined to be prepared.

By 1811, war with the U.S. seemed imminent, and when the Lt.-Governor of Upper Canada, Francis Gore, was obliged to be absent, Brock was promoted to the rank of Major-General, and appointed provisional Lt.-Governor of Upper Canada. he was determined that his "province" would be prepared for the war he felt sure was coming. His superiors, however, were determined that he would not have the resources needed to make a pre-emptive strike against the Americans, which they were convinced was his intention.

Brock pestered Governor Prevost for supplies and men to defend his frontier. Prevost responded with very little and an admonishment that what he did supply was not to be used in any way "unless they were solely calculated to strengthen a defensive position."[24] Tied up with administrative duties in his office as Lt.-Governor in York, Brock expressed his opinions and doubts about the loyalty — and the will to fight — of many of Canada's settlers.

In May he wrote, "The population, believe me, is essentially bad ... A full belief possesses them all that this province must inevitably succumb."[25] While Brock was trying as Governor to instill loyalty in the local people, others were openly advising the settlers not to join any militia units or take part in any way in any fighting. A frustrated Brock reported: "A petition has already been carried to Genl. Hull signed by many inhabitants about Westminster inviting him to advance with a promise to join him — What in the name of heaven can be done with such a vile population?"[26]

The General was a soldier and felt that he should be soldiering, not governing an apathetic population who did not seem willing to defend their own lands and homes. He wanted to be in Spain or France, fighting with the Duke of Wellington, earning accolades and promotions, not stuck in an administrative job in the backwoods of Upper Canada. He

had little love for Upper Canada or its people. a true English-
man, he hated the "provinces," vacillating bureaucrats, mud-
dling militias and native "savages." At least in Montreal he
could enjoy good food and passable wine, a semblance of
sophisticated society, and some of the niceties of life which
he had grown accustomed to expect. In Upper Canada he
suffered from a lack of all the things he wanted, and a surplus
of all the things he didn't want. As one observer noted, Brock
"could hardly wait to shake the Canadian mud from his
boots and bid goodbye forever to York, Fort George, Quebec,
and all the stuffy garrison towns between."[27]

When the time to stand up and be counted came in July,
1812, Brock was the first one to rise. By this time he had been
seeking — and had been granted — permission to leave
Canada, but with the outbreak of war chose to stay. He wrote
his brother in England that month; "Most of the people have
lost all confidence. I, however, speak loud and look big."[28]

Whatever his reason for staying, whether it was out of a
true sense of duty, or in recognition that the "small" war in
America was the only one he was going to get into very soon,
is a matter of speculation. But once he'd committed himself,
he threw himself headlong into the fray. Without waiting for
orders from — or having consultations with — Quebec, he
took the offensive on the Niagara frontier. He sent a force to
take Fort Michilimackinac on Lake Huron, and he himself
marched on Fort Detroit. He took both American positions
virtually without firing a shot.

But to Brock there was no glory in a "bloodless" victory.
He longed for the action and drama that would elevate him
in the eyes of his superiors and the public. On October 13,
1812, he got his chance, and charged headlong into battle —
and into the pages of history — at Queenston Heights. Today
an impressive monument marks Brock's gravesite, and he is

Today, this impressive 190 foot monument marks the site of Brock's final resting place on Queenston Heights, very near the site of the original 1824 tower. Begun in 1853, it was completed three years later at a cost of $40,000.

commemorated as the "first hero of Canada," the saviour of the country, who stood up to the bullying and blustering Americans.

Brock was firstly, and simply, a soldier. He knew his duty and did it. It was obvious someone had to lead the often apathetic, vacillating and at times even treasonous civilians of the Upper Canadian province. Even if Brock was somewhat vain and glory-seeking, this in no way diminishes his courage or the not often found quality of true leadership. It is only fitting that Canadians today revere his memory, yet perhaps temper their pride with the fact that had they been as patriotic and ready to serve as were many of the "adopted" sons of the country, Canada itself may have borne some of its own true, genuine heroes.

Endnotes:

1. Saunders; op. cit., p. 37.
2. Ibid.
3. Ibid, p. 36.
4. Raddal; op. cit., p. 30.
5. Saunders; op. cit., p. 23.
6. Berton; op. cit., p. 260.
7. Saunders, op. cit., p. 2.
8. Ibid.
9. Berton; op. cit., p. 260. Many of the regular Army troops were savage at him; some of them smashed their muskets in rage, others, even more incensed, tried to kill him that night by shooting into his tent.
10. Raddal; op. cit., p. 209. One observer later summed up Gen. Smyth's failure and fiasco at Fort Erie by saying, "Smyth, by the time it was light enough for the British to see him, had 1,500 men in boats, who all wanted to go back, and 3,000 on shore, who all refused to go forward." Of Smyth's Generalship even American newspapers wrote, "...Smyth must be added to the catalogue of infamy...there never was an expedition better planned...nothing failed but the general...for never was a nation cursed with worse generals than the American people seem to have been...Smyth was denounced and hooted through the streets of Buffalo (New York)."
11. Raddal; op. cit., p. 215.
12. Saunders; op. cit., p. 11. (Vol. 50, No. 3, Dec. 1950. N.Q.)
13. Berton; op. cit., p. 289.
14. Berton; op. cit., p. 292-293. Lt. Rolette is said to have had such a headache at the time of the march, that his commanding officer tried to persuade him to stay behind. Rolette told him to tie a red bandanna tightly around his head and he would be alright. Major Reynolds did so and Rolette is said to have commented: "I am better already," and started off with his detachment.
15. Ibid, page 294. Lt. Rolette was knocked senseless by the musket ball to his head, but otherwise unhurt. The thick bandanna he had wrapped around his head that morning absorbed the impact of the ball and thus saved his life. Second Lt. Irvine was also shot in the heel but carried on with his Newfoundlanders to rescue the cannon.
16. Raddal; op. cit., p. 216. Procter's hesitancy had cost him the lives of 182 British soldiers. Winchester's losses were complete. Of his 1,000 men, 536 were taken prisoner, thirty-three were missing and nearly 400 dead — many of them massacred by the Indians even after they had surrendered and been taken prisoner. When the bloody scene was over, nearly 400 American scalps dangled from the war-belts of the Indians.
17. Saunders; op. cit., p. 9. The non-commissioned officers of the Newfoundland Regiment — the sergeants and corporals — were deemed experienced and capable enough of leading their men on the battlefield without an officer. As one observer commented, "The Newfoundlanders were left with no officers; but every private here, was, to paraphrase Bonaparte, 'Carrying an officer's baton in his knapsack'."
18. Ibid, p. 10.
19. Raddall; op. cit., p. 205.
20. Calvert, Brig. Michael and Brig. Michael Young; *A Dictionary of Battles: 1715-1815*. p. 211.

21. Ibid. p. 208.
22. Berton; *The Invasion of Canada*. p. 133.
23. Ibid.
24. Dyer, Gwynne; op. cit., p. 74.
25. Ibid.
26. Berton; op. cit., p. 143.
27. Ibid. p. 253.
28. Dyer; op. cit., p. 74.

CHAPTER SEVEN

Fort York Falls and Fort Amherstburg Fails

N MARCH 1, 1813 the commander of the British forces at Kingston received orders to move the headquarters of the Royal Newfoundland Regiment to York, the provincial capital of Upper Canada. "The headquarters of the Royal Newfoundland Regiment," the orders read, "is to be removed to York. Colonel Pearson will give you the necessary orders and instructions for Lt. Col. Heathcote proceeding with such proportion of the Regiment now at Kingston as can be spared from the marine service of that port..."[1]

Obviously not all of the Regiment was to be moved as their skill as seamen was greatly recognized as badly needed to be "marines" in the provincial marine service. During the early weeks of March, Heathcote moved quickly to consolidate his Newfoundlanders at York. He left the "Flanking" Company under Captain Whelan at Fort Erie where it was sorely needed and the company under Captain Mockler at Fort Amherstburg were cut off by the deep freeze of winter.

While Heathcote was preparing his new headquarters, Captain Whelan and his small company at Fort Erie were defending their old ones. On St. Patrick's Day the Americans decided to celebrate by bombarding the British fort. Two batteries set up below the fort returned the American's fire. One was commanded by Captain Whelan with one 12-pounder and the other with two 3-pounders was under Lt. Garden while the company of Newfoundland Fencibles under Major Ormsby stood in readiness to repel any infantry attack from Black Rock across the Niagara River.

The American shelling killed one of the Newfoundlanders and wounded two others, but the return fire of Whelan and Garden showed them that the Irish Newfoundlanders were also ready to celebrate their patron Saint's day with more gusto and even more accuracy. The Newfoundland gunners knocked out three of the American batteries and the celebration was over.[2]

Following this "celebration" at Fort Erie, the commander at Fort York, Lt. Col. Myers, wrote headquarters at Niagara (on the Lake) that he felt the defences of the Niagara River were tenuous and should not be unduly weakened by removing the Royal Newfoundland Regiment from Kingston to York. Myers wrote, "The line from Fort George to Fort Erie can but ill spare the temporary loss of them (R.N.R); in the meantime the best distribution possible of what is left will be made."[3]

Myers proved to be half right and headquarters at Niagara half wrong. The Americans had planned a spring offensive across Lake Ontario which initially was to attack Kingston and then York and finally the Niagara River. Some of the American commanders overestimated the British strength at Kingston and insisted on a first strike at York which they knew to be undermanned and badly fortified. The transfer of the Newfoundland Regiment increased the garrison there by about 100 men and added several more cannon which General Sheaffe described as "two complete 12-pounders and two old condemned guns" which had been repaired and mounted under the direction of Lieutenant Ignouville of the Royal Newfoundland Regiment whom Sheaffe had appointed Assistant Engineer.[4]

The reason for the American change of plans is not entirely clear but it may be simply that they needed to start the new year of offensives with a striking victory that would boost the morale of the army and the country who had seen nothing but a dismal, costly and embarrassing string of defeats during 1812. Striking at York and capturing it would be a great morale booster. Although it was smaller than Kingston and not as well defended, it was the seat of the provincial government of Upper Canada.

A member of the Royal Newfoundland Regiment stationed there in 1813, P. Finan, described York as "a pleasant little town, the houses generally of wood, and containing some good shops. Being the seat of government of the upper province, it has a house of assembly, court house, etc. It is situated at the lower end of a long bay formed by a narrow peninsula stretching up the lake...On the extremity of this, called Gibraltar Point, stands a lighthouse, and exactly opposite it, on the mainland, the garrison is situated, where we reside."[5]

On April 26, 1813 fourteen American warships towing transport boats for 1700 troops began sailing across Lake Ontario bound for York under command of Major General Henry Dearborn. His two field commanders were Major Benjamin Forsyth commanding two battalions of American riflemen and General Zebulon Pike who led the regular Army troops. York was defended by about 800 men; 300 York militiamen, about fifty Indians, and 450 regulars including a company of the Glengarry Fencibles, two companies of the 8th (King's) Regiment, and two understrength companies of

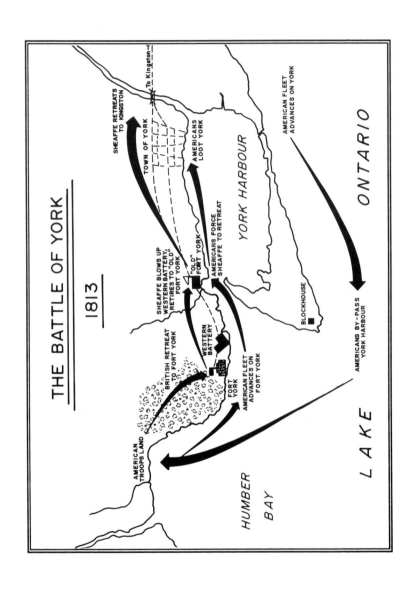

THE BATTLE OF YORK

1813

AMERICAN TROOPS LAND

BRITISH RETREAT TO FORT YORK

SHEAFFE BLOWS UP WESTERN BATTERY, RETIRES TO "OLD" FORT YORK

SHEAFFE RETREATS TO KINGSTON

To Kingston

TOWN OF YORK

AMERICANS LOOT YORK

AMERICAN FLEET ADVANCES ON YORK

YORK HARBOUR

AMERICANS FORCE SHEAFFE TO RETREAT

"OLD" FORT YORK

WESTERN BATTERY

FORT YORK

AMERICAN FLEET ADVANCES ON FORT YORK

BLOCKHOUSE

AMERICANS BY-PASS YORK HARBOUR

ONTARIO

LAKE

HUMBER BAY

the Royal Newfoundland Regiment under Heathcote who had just arrived from Kingston.[6]

At dawn on the following day the American fleet was sighted by sentries and the signal was given of the impending attack. But the British could not tell just what was being attacked. The Americans bypassed York and its harbour and continued westward up the lake. The British could not tell where they were going to land. They were encountering unfavourable winds and had trouble making a landing. The attackers were finally able to land on a beach in Humber Bay, several miles west of York. Still, they had trouble approaching the shore in a calm and the delay gave Sheaffe time to send a company of the 8th grenadiers to help the Indians try to stop them on the beaches. The grenadiers' and Indians' musket fire proved effective enough on the American troop transports that Forsyth's frontiersmen put down their oars and picked up their rifles to cover their landing.

Unable to hold the swarming riflemen, the British and Indians retreated into the woods east of the landing site and prepared to engage them in a sniper's shootout. The Newfoundland companies and the Glengarries were rushed forward to support them. It was Sheaffe's intention for them to make a bayonet charge, but along the way to the woods the Glengarries got lost. The Newfoundlanders found themselves alone with only the small company of grenadiers and a handful of the Indians who had not scattered in the face of the American onslaught.[7]

A bayonet charge was now out of the question and the Newfoundlanders and remaining redcoats had no choice but to retreat deeper into the woods and try to slow the Americans who by now had landed in such numbers that they outnumbered the British advance guard by more than two to one. The retreating Newfoundlanders and grenadiers fought

stubbornly in the woods for half an hour before finally
withdrawing to their main lines. They suffered heavy casualties; thirty-six of their ranks, including one officer, were
killed, wounded or captured.[8]

The overwhelmed British now decided to retreat entirely
from their advance position to the protection of their guns at
the "Western Battery" at the mouth of York harbour. The tiny
"Fort" York itself was not defensible — indeed there was
little to defend. At the Western Battery the British began to
regroup and bring their big guns into play. For a short time it
began to look as if they could make a stand. Then, fate dealt
the redcoats another unlucky hand.

One of the gunners dropped his lighted fuse into a port-
able powder magazine. The explosion blew the cannons off
their carriages and, as the Newfoundlander Finan later
wrote, "Every man in the battery was blown into the air, and
the 'dissection' of the great part of their bodies was incon-
ceivably shocking!"[9]

The blast demoralized the British defenders and gave the
Americans a fresh opportunity to advance. All their ground
forces were now landed and steadily advancing on the town.
The U.S. ships had now also entered the harbour and began
pounding the British flanks with heavy 32-pounder cannon
shot. Sheaffe saw only two options — retreat or surrender.
He decided to save his force to fight another day and chose
the former. But he was determined to leave the Americans
nothing of use.

He decided to blow up Fort York which housed a huge
powder magazine built of stone and mortar, thus depriving
the Americans of its great store of powder and shot. The
magazine contained 500 barrels of gunpowder and hundreds
of shells and cannon shot.

The magazine blew up like a gigantic bomb, belching cannon shot, brick, mortar and stones over an area more than 300 feet in diameter. Private Finan of the Royal Newfoundland Regiment again was an eye witness to the incident. "...an immense cloud," he recorded, "...A great confused mass of smoke, timber, earth,...rose, in a most majestic manner, it assumed the shape of a vast balloon."[10] The enormous explosion killed fifty-two of the Americans and injured 180 others. Among the dead was the American leader Zebulon Pike. The blast also killed dozens of the British soldiers, even wounding Sheaffe's aid, whose horse was killed under him. Sheaffe had ordered the detonation of the magazine too early.[11]

With his forces regrouped east of York, Sheaffe paused to survey the situation. The bombastic blast had thrown the Americans into chaos and some thought that if he had mounted a stiff counter-attack at that moment "our rallied force would have routed the enemy, divided and panic-stricken by the catastrophe."[12]

Sheaffe called his officers together for a quick consult-ation, asking for opinions. Only one of them gave one. Major Heathcote of the Royal Newfoundland Regiment said he "was of the opinion to have another fight."[13] Sheaffe how-ever did not take the Newfoundlander's advice and ordered his force to retreat to Kingston forthwith.

While the Americans were successfully attacking Fort York on the eastern Niagara frontier, the British were unsuc-cessfully attacking Fort Meigs on the western Detroit fron-tier. While Procter feverishly made plans for a second attack on Fort Meigs, Harrisson fervently hoped for reinforce-ments. Both commanders had to wait for spring. Harrisson's help under command of General Green Clay were bogged down in heavy snow and Procter could not move his artillery for the same reason. Spring came first however, for Procter and the British.

By early April, he was joined by the Shawnee Chief Tecumseh, who had just recovered from an illness, and over 1,000 Indian warriors. Procter had managed to raise up a force of 400 Canadian militia to augment his 500 regulars and with Tecumseh's Indians hoped to march on Fort Meigs with a force of nearly 2,000 men. He believed he would be facing a force of less than half that size but Harrisson's help was close at hand.

Near the end of the month Procter had his men settled in at the foot of the Maumee Falls just below Fort Meigs and had set up two batteries of guns, one on each side of the river, to pound the American stockade. Tecumseh's warriors were sent across the river to harass the fort at close range with musket fire. On May 1st, Procter began his siege of Fort Meigs. For four days his guns bombarded the American post, but Harrisson refused to surrender. On the fourth day the relief he was expecting from upriver arrived in the person of General Green Clay and 1,200 Kentucky and Ohio frontiersmen. Harrisson instructed Clay to split his force and land the bulk of them on the north side of the river then strike through the country and surprise the British batteries on their flanks. The rest of Clay's force was to land on the south side of the river, engage and route Tecumseh's Indians, fight their way into the fort to join forces with Harrisson's men, who would then march out en masse and engage the British force.[14]

For a time it seemed that Harrisson's strategy would work. General Clay's forces succeeded in surprising the British batteries and quickly captured one of their gun positions. Instead of holding their ground and securing their position, the green American militiamen pushed towards the main British camp. Tecumseh and his warriors quickly

Photo: Nicholson — *The Fighting Newfoundlander*

Monument in Toronto commemorating those who died, including members of the Royal Newfoundland Regiment, in the defence of "York" in the War of 1812.

crossed the river, some in canoes, others swimming, and attacked Clay's men in the flanks. As the Americans faltered, Captain Peter Chambers of the 14th Regiment saw a chance to recapture the silenced cannon.

Dropping his sword, he grabbed up a bayoneted musket of a fallen comrade and yelled, "Who will follow me and

retake that battery?" Lt. LeBreton of the Royal Newfoundland Regiment, along with Lt. Garden — who had recently
returned from the St. "Paddy's" Day celebration at Fort Erie
and was now commanding one of the artillery batteries —
rushed forward with him. Chambers, LeBreton, Garden and
a squad of Newfoundlanders charged the captured gun
position with fixed bayonets.

Although greatly outnumbered in their gallant charge,
one observer recounted, "Those on the scene saw no reason
why the whole of Chamber's band should not have been
annihilated. They retook the battery and drove the enemy
into their boats."[15]

While Clay's men were being soundly routed on the
north side of the river, Harrisson rallied forth from the fort
with his troops and attacked the second British battery and
remaining Indian force that had not gone to Procter's aid.
Harrisson captured the guns, scattering the Indians, but soon
learned that Clay's men were in retreat and he himself would
soon be in peril. He quickly retreated back behind the strong
palisades of Fort Meigs.

The Battle of Maumee Falls was a disaster for the Americans. Of 800 men Clay led into battle 200 were killed, 450
taken prisoner, while only 150 escaped to join Harrisson
inside the safe walls of Fort Meigs. The British losses were
less, but still very costly. They lost 101 men killed and several
taken prisoner. Procter could not hope to replace his casualties; Harrisson had an almost endless supply of reinforcements from the south. Among the British casualties were a
drummer and two privates of the Royal Newfoundland
Regiment killed, one wounded and one taken prisoner.[16]

During the next two days an unofficial truce was observed by the combatants as wounded were cared for and
prisoners exchanged. Procter was eager to continue his siege

as he had the Americans bottled up in the fort and knew no further reinforcements would arrive for some time. He felt confident after his stunning victory that the siege could not last long. The Indians and militia had a different opinion. For the militia there was a spring ploughing to be done, and for the Indians booty to be carried back to their camps and victory celebrations to be held. Left with only his badly decimated regulars and a handful of Tecumseh's warriors, Procter realized it was useless to lay siege to a fort that held more than three times his numbers.[17]

On May 7th, Procter loaded his men and cannon aboard his bateaux and the "Boat Brigade" of the Royal Newfoundland Regiment ferried all back across Lake Erie to their base at Fort Amherstburg. In his report to Governor Provost on May 14th, General Procter highly commended the men of the Royal Newfoundland Regiment. "Besides my obligation to Captain Chambers," he wrote, "I have to notice his gallant conduct in attacking the enemy near the batteries, on which he was well supported by Lt. LeBreton of the Royal Newfoundland Regiment... Lieut. LeBreton by his unswerving exertion rendered essential service. The Royal Artillery were well assisted by the Royal Newfoundland Regiment as additional gunners under Lieut. Garden...To Captain Mockler of the Royal Newfoundland Regiment, who acted as my aide-de-camp, I am much indebted for the assistance he afforded me."[18]

PROFILE; THE "COLOURS" OF THE REGIMENT: HONOUR DENIED

The "colours," or flag, of the Royal Newfoundland Regiment, granted to them in 1806 by King George III and their emblem until 1816 when the Regiment was disbanded, has a "colourful" history of its own. When Newfoundland was granted permission to raise a company of "Fencibles"— soldiers to be used for defence only — in 1804 they were quickly raised, trained and moulded into a loyal and disciplined force within two years. In 1806 they were conferred the title "Royal" by his majesty and with this designation came the right and privilege to bear their own colours.

That year the Regiment's nearly 600 men were transferred from Newfoundland to continental North America to serve in essentially a "foreign" land as protectors of the King's empire. They saw duty from the east in Halifax, through Quebec and Ontario, and as far west as the Mississippi River in present day Wisconsin, U.S.A. At the outbreak of war between Britain and the United States in 1812, most of the Royal Newfoundland Regiment was stationed in Quebec but were quickly dispersed westward along the Canadian-American frontier along the Great Lakes in "Upper Canada."

Until now, the Regiment had operated as a whole unit from one headquarters but that now changed with the nature of the duties assigned to the men from Newfoundland. The Regiment was split into small companies and detachments that would see duty in every military capacity both on land and sea. As a consequence of this duty and the scattering of the Regiment that it would require, Major Rowland Heathcote, commander of the Regiment received a General Order from the Adjutant-General at Quebec on July 24, 1812 which stated: "In consequence of the nature of service required from the Royal Newfoundland Regiment necessarily subdividing that Corps into small Detachments, Major Heathcote is directed to leave the Colours of the Regiment in this Garrison, to be lodged in the Ordnance Armoury."[19]

There, the colours of the Regiment languished until September of 1815, when the last members of the Corps were transferred back to Newfoundland after more than three years of farflung service on mainland North America in battles which they fought under the colours of some other regiment. In the War of 1812, the Royal Newfoundland Regiment saw action in almost every major engagement in Upper Canada. Its men fought and died in the battles at Fort Detroit, Fort Erie (in November, 1812 and again in March of 1813), Frenchtown, Ogdensburg, York, Sackett's Harbour, Fort George, the siege of Fort Meigs, Fort Stephenson, the Battle of Lake Erie, Moraviantown on the Thames, Chrysler's Farm, Stoney Creek, Fort Mackinac, the "battle" of Lake Huron, and at Fort McKay at Prairie du Chien on the Mississippi River.[20]

In all of these and numerous other skirmishes and engagements not classified as "battles," the men of the Royal Newfoundland Regiment never once had the honour of, or felt the pride of, marching onto the field of battle under their own colours. Time after time, in all of the "major" battles and "minor" skirmishes in which the Regiment took part, its officers and men were repeatedly commended to their superiors for their conduct and bravery under fire. For their valour during the War of 1812, members of the Regiment received seven "General Service Medals" with clasps, belatedly struck by Queen Victoria in 1847 in recognition of the heroic actions of the men who fought in the War of 1812-1814.[21]

In 1815, the Royal Newfoundland Regiment was repatriated to its homeland colony. Maj. Heathcote and the main portion of the Regiment had returned to the island in the summer, but his second-in-command, Major Elias Pipon had remained in Quebec to gather up the last remnants of the Regiment which included the Mississippi Volunteers and the prisoners of war from Ohio and Kentucky. With the last of his Regiment gathered, Pipon set sail for home, taking with him the colours of the Regiment.[22]

When the Regiment was disbanded in 1816, Major Pipon retired from the Army and returned to his home in Jersey, taking the colours of the Royal Newfoundland Regiment with him. They remained in obscurity for sixty-five years, possibly residing in the home of Pipon, until 1882 when they were presented to St. Brelades' Church in Jersey by Major Pipon's nephew, P.G. Pipon, himself a Major-General in the British Army.[23]

There, the colours of the Regiment rested for almost forty years, a testament to the valour of men on the other side of the Atlantic Ocean who did not even have the honour of fighting under it. Shortly after the First World War, a group of Newfoundland tourists who visited the church on the Channel Islands, recognized the flag of the Newfoundlanders who had fought and died for Canada and Britain over 100 years earlier and took back the news of their discovery to Newfoundland.

The Newfoundland Historical Society of the day under the auspices of H.W. LeMessurier and H.F. Shortis, two very keen conservationists of Newfoundland history, persuaded the Newfoundland Government to help in "repatriating" the colours. Together they succeeded in persuading the Jersey authorities to allow the flags to be returned to Newfoundland and in their place presented the city of Jersey with a

Photo: *The Fighting Newfoundlander*

Regimental Flag (Colours) of the Royal Newfoundland Regiment
in the War of 1812 – 1814

commemorative plaque to memorialize the resting place of
the Regiment's relics for over 100 years.

The Regimental colours of the Royal Newfoundland
Regiment were returned to Newfoundland in 1922, and officially turned over to the government of the island on June 3,
1922, the birthday of King George V of England. The flags
were turned over to the care of the Newfoundland Museum
in a ceremony with great pomp, that was attended by the
Governor of Newfoundland, Sir Charles A. Harris, Church
and State officials, members of the Historical Society and
educational institutions, and a honour guard of veterans of
the "Blue Puttees," the Royal Newfoundland Regiment of
the First World War.[24]

The Historical Society of Newfoundland
has the honour to invite

Miss Mollie White,
Bishop Spencer College,

to be present at the ceremony attendant upon the receipt of
two flags of the Royal Newfoundland Regiment of the
eighteenth century which, fully one hundred years after their
departure from Newfoundland, have been returned to this
Country through the efforts of the Historical Society of Newfoundland, by the good offices of the High Commissioner and
the generosity of the authorities of St. Brelade's Church, Jersey.

The ceremony will take place on the Birthday of His Majesty
King George V, June 3rd, 1922, at 3 p.m. o'clock,
in the Museum.

His Excellency the Governor Sir Charles Alexander Harris,
K.C.M.G., C.B., C.V.O., will preside at the function.

H. W. LeMessurier, President.

Kindly show this
card at the door.

Warwick Smith, Rec.-Secretary,

R.S.V.P.

Personalized invitation sent to citizens of Newfoundland to attend the ceremony of repatriation of
the "colours" — from Jersey, England — of the Royal Newfoundland Regiment of the War of 1812-
1814.

Home at last, the flag that had been forgotten about for
more than 100 years, entered an even more "unmemorable"
period. In 1935, the Memorial Museum was confiscated as
office space for the new Commission of Government and its
treasures and relics scattered to diverse "holding pens"
around the city. Many of the artifacts were badly treated or
carelessly stored, some — including the colours of the Royal
Newfoundland Regiment — were even ill-used. The flag was
hung, in its fragile state, in the Assembly Hall of Memorial
College on Merrymeeting Road, but years later it was decided to store it in the vault of the College for safe keeping.
There, it seems, it was forgotten once again throughout the

Second World War and through the years during the fight for Confederation.

When the Naval and Military Museum was set up in Confederation Building, its curator, David Webber set out to find the Regiment's colours. He traced them to Memorial College, but the old vault was so seized up it took an acetylene torch to open it. The flags however were not there. Webber eventually located them in the property room of Memorial University "in the last stages of disintegration."[25] They had been in "use" for some time as a prop or set decoration by mindless, or uncaring, aspiring thespians of the artistic throngs, who, it is hoped, were merely ignorant and not desecrating.

Today, the relics of the colours of the Royal Newfoundland Regiment of 1812-1814 are safely stored by the successors of the tradition of the original regiments, the present day Royal Newfoundland Regiment, who ensure them an honourable, if not immortal, preservation. Hopefully, the faded and frail colours await a restoration that will once again, perhaps allow them to be displayed to the new generations of sons and daughters of the brave and loyal men of the Royal Newfoundland Regiments that helped keep Canada for Canadians.

Endnotes:

1. Harrington, Michael F.; "Newfoundlanders Defended Toronto in 1813." *Evening Telegram*. July 4, 1988.
2. Nicholson, Col. G.W.L.; *The Fighting Newfoundlanders*, p. 74.
3. Saunders; op. cit., p. 9.
4. Harrington; op. cit.
5. Stanley, George F.G.; *The War of 1812*, p. 169.
6. Ibid.
7. Berton, Pierre; *Flames Across The Border*, p. 48. Of the 1219 grenadiers of the 8th (King's) Regiment that had been sent to support the Indians at the landing site only thirty remained by the time the Royal Newfoundland Companies arrived to support them.
8. Nicholson; op. cit., p. 76. At the Battle of York the Royal Newfoundland Regiment saw one of its officers and sixteen other ranks—many of whom were wounded—taken prisoner by the Americans, and twelve others were killed and seven more wounded who were safely carried from the battlefield.
9. Stanley; op. cit., p. 172.
10. Ibid, p. 173.
11. Raddall; op. cit., p. 242.
12. Saunders; op. cit., p. 11.
13. Ibid. After the capture of York, the Americans proceeded to destroy the town. They burned the parliament buildings with its library, law courts, and record offices of the Houses of Assembly. They turned prisoners loose and told them to help themselves. Merchants as well as private citizens were robbed and looted, and churches and public buildings pillaged. A reason given for this savage destruction is that a scalp was found in an office of a public official. The Americans had long believed—erroneously—that the British were paying their Indian allies a bounty for American scalps, and that they now had proof. When the Americans withdrew from York about a week later, some of the citizens who had been looted approached Dearborn for compensation. The American commander compensated them, but with money he had confiscated from the provincial treasury. The following year when the British invaded Washington D.C. they too burned the American capital to the ground in revenge.
14. Stanley; op. cit., p. 150.
15. Berton; op. cit., p. 121.
16. Saunders; op. cit., p. 15.
17. Nicholson; op. cit., p. 73.
18. Saunders, op. cit., p. 16.
19. Nicholson; op. cit., p. 66.
20. Saunders, Dr. Robert; "When Newfoundland Helped Save Canada." *Newfoundland Quarterly*. Vol. 50, No. 1, Dec. 1950, p. 11.
21. Stanley; op. cit., p. 426.
22. Nicholson; op. cit., p. 85.
23. Harrington, Michael; "The Sad Fate of Regimental Flags." *The Evening Telegram*, Jan. 10, 1983.
24. Stanley, George F.G.; *The War of 1812*, p. 169.
25. Ibid.

CHAPTER EIGHT

Retreat on the Canadian Frontier

OLLOWING THEIR VICTORY AT YORK the Americans pressed on with their plans to capture the Niagara frontier. During the weeks of May, Dearborn had the troops from York returned to Fort Niagara and sent for reinforcements from Sackett's Harbour and other posts south in New York and Ohio. By May 24th, he had amassed 6,000 troops at the fort in preparation for an attack on Fort George.

Across the Niagara at Fort George, Brigadier General John Vincent who had assumed command from Sheaffe following the loss of York, had with him about 1,300 regulars and militia, and about fifty Indians at his disposal. Among the regulars were two companies of the Royal Newfoundland Regiment, a company of the Glengarries, and companies of the 41st, 49th and 8th Regiments. Vincent faced a force more than three times his number and knew he had no hope of reinforcement. The Americans controlled the lake, and he could expect no help from Procter in the west.[1]

On May 25th, the Americans began shelling Fort George from Fort Niagara. Shot, heated red-hot in foundry furnaces, rained down on the British fort and soon had all the wooden buildings in the post aflame. The fires kept the British occupied for the entire day, all the while they were expecting the

American attack. It didn't come until the following day when the U.S. ships attempted to land their troops in a dense fog west of the fort. But the fog lifted as the ships pulled into position and Vincent hurriedly rushed the Newfoundland companies under command of Captain William Winter, and the Glengarries along with the Indians, to intercept them on the beach about two miles west of the fort.

National Portrait Gallery, Smithsonian Institute

The Newfoundlanders took up a position in a ravine overlooking the beach and waited for the first wave of attackers. Leading them was Colonel Winfield Scott, a big man who stood over six feet five inches tall making a big target. As he led the first wave of his men ashore and began up the muddy, slippery riverbank the Newfoundlanders scrambled from their cover in the ravine to meet them.

Brig.-General Winfield Scott, commander of the American Troops at the battle of Fort George.

One of them made a bayonet thrust at Scott, but the American commander slipped on the mud and fell back into the water. If Scott had ever made a slip in his life this was probably the most important one.[2]

The British beat back the first assault and as the Americans regrouped on the shoreline their ships began to rake the Redcoats with grapeshot. They took heavy casualties and were forced to withdraw towards Fort George. Scott and his Bluecoats now gained the landing site and secured the way for the following waves of troops. The Newfoundlanders and Glengarries held up in a second ravine about a mile from the fort and attempted to halt the American advance. But their less than 200 number complement had by now been cut by more than half and hundreds of American troops were now ashore and rushing their position.

As one observer reported, "Despite the dreadful losses they suffered by grape and round shot from the enemy's vessels, they drove them back several times...The British force lost about two-thirds of their strength...of the 200 Glengarry and Newfoundland Regiments 114 were placed hors de combat (casualties)."[3]

Public Archives of Nova Scotia

Lt.-Col. John Harvey who led the British in a surprise night attack against the Americans at Stoney Creek, later became Governor of Newfoundland

Colonel Harvey and the 49th soon arrived to support the Newfoundlanders but by then the Americans had landed their field artillery and forced the British to retreat once again into a third position just hundreds of yards outside Fort George. It was now about noon and Vincent learned that a force of the enemy was attempting to flank the fort and cut off any chance of flight. The British commander acted quickly to save his force. He ordered the guns spiked and the fort abandoned, which by now consisted merely of a few burned buildings and battered ramparts.

He sent word to Lt. Col Bisshopp at Fort Erie and Major Ormsby at Chippewa to evacuate their posts and rendezvous with his men at Beaver Dams, a supply depot about fifteen miles west of the Niagara River. While Vincent hurriedly

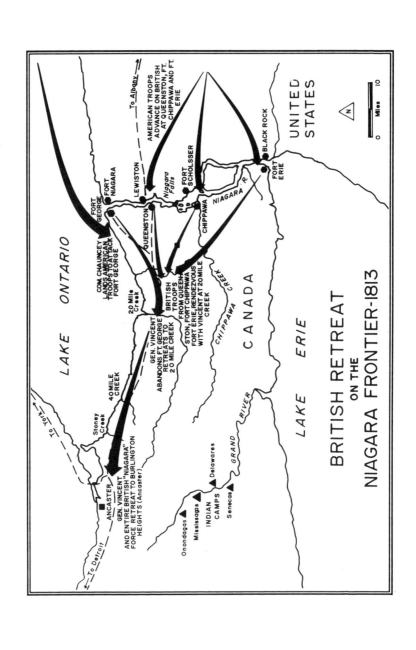

UNITED STATES

LAKE ONTARIO

CANADA

LAKE ERIE

N

0 Miles 10

To Albany

AMERICAN TROOPS ADVANCE ON BRITISH AT QUEENSTON, FT. CHIPPAWA AND FT. ERIE

FORT NIAGARA

LEWISTON

Niagara Falls

FORT SCHOLSSER

BLACK ROCK

FORT GEORGE

NIAGARA R.

FORT ERIE

QUEENSTON

CHIPPAWA

COM CHAUNCEY LANDS AMERICAN TROOPS TO ATTACK FORT GEORGE

20 Mile Creek

BRITISH TROOPS FROM QUEENSTON, FORT CHIPPAWA FORT ERIE, RENDEZVOUS WITH VINCENT AT 20 MILE CREEK

CHIPPAWA CREEK

GEN. VINCENT ABANDONS FT. GEORGE RETREATS TO 20 MILE CREEK

40 MILE CREEK

Stoney Creek

GRAND RIVER

To York

ANCASTER

GEN. VINCENT AND ENTIRE BRITISH "NIAGARA" FORCE RETREAT TO BURLINGTON HEIGHTS (Ancaster)

To Detroit

Onondagas

Mississagas

Delawares

INDIAN CAMPS

Senecas

BRITISH RETREAT
ON THE
NIAGARA FRONTIER-1813

gathered up anything of use, he had the Newfoundland and Glengarry regiments fight a delaying action with the advancing enemy. Adjutant General Baynes reported that, "After evacuating Fort George and falling back to Queenston Heights, General Vincent reports that the movements were ably covered by the companies of the Glengarry...strengthened by a detachment of the Royal Newfoundland Regiment."[4]

When all his forces from along the Niagara River were grouped at Queenston, Vincent began his hasty, but orderly retreat towards the head of Lake Ontario. At Beaver Dams he paused to wait for Col. Bisshopp and Capt. Whelan and his companies of the Royal Newfoundland Regiment coming from Fort Erie.

While Vincent and his Redcoats retreated, the Americans were busy securing their captured fort on the Niagara and preparing a pursuit of the British. The day after the fall of Fort George, Governor Prevost, who was now in Kingston, decided to make a fast strike at Sackett's Harbour on the American side of Lake Ontario at its eastern end. Sackett's Harbour was an American shipbuilding site and was busy building vessels for a major U.S. offensive later that year. What bothered Prévost and the British was that the Americans were building ships faster than they themselves were. Sackett's Harbour was also the headquarters of the American fleet on Lake Ontario under command of Commodore Chauncey who was now at Fort George with all his ships having transported the 6,000 American troops to the Niagara for the assault.

Prevost's attack was to be a combined Army-Navy action. In command of the ships would be recently arrived Royal Navy Commodore Sir James Yeo. Prevost had 750 British regulars and Canadian militia, and a war party of

Indians under his command. Yeo had three Royal Navy warships, the *Prince Regent,* the *Royal George,* and the *Earl of Moira* under his command. All of the 230 members of the Royal Newfoundland Regiment which were still stationed at Kingston were assigned duty as "marines" aboard Yeo's ships. The *Royal George* was manned by 123 of them, the *Prince Regent* with fifty-three, and the *Earl of Moira* had fifty-four men.[5]

On the morning that Fort George was being attacked by Dearborn, Prevost took advantage of Chauncey's absence from Sackett's Harbour and set sail from Kingston with Yeo's three ships towing thirty-three landing boats, and a small flotilla of canoes filled with Indians. Early the next morning as they neared the target and the regulars and Newfoundland marines were piling aboard their landing boats Prevost ordered them back aboard ship. Nineteen American troop boats were sighted moving up the lake shore and Prevost hesitated. His moment of indecision cost him his edge of surprise.

Whatever his reason, he was soon convinced by the hasty retreat of the American boats that he was in no danger of attack. A boatload of the Newfoundland "marines" and the swift Indian canoes were sent in pursuit. The "marines" and Indians succeeded in cutting off and capturing twelve of the boats but seven of them escaped to the safety of Sackett's Harbour with the news of the impending British attack.

Still Prevost hesitated. By the time he decided to attack on the morning of May 29th, the commander of the American garrison had gathered 1,300 regular soldiers and New York militia to defend the shipyard. The smaller British force landed and attacked with a fury that saw the New York militia break after firing only one volley. Unable to regroup his men, the American commander put his post to the torch.

He set fire to the barracks, storehouses, and shipyard, as well as the ship *Duke of Glouster*, a British vessel captured at York and their own as yet unfinished warship *General Pike*.[6]

By the time Prevost reached the burning shipyard the Americans had withdrawn to the town of Sackett's Harbour. Again the Governor hesitated. He had only about 450 of his force of 750 left for another attack. He had lost over 260 casualties and the others were scattered in the confusion. As Prevost vacillated some of his officers urged him to press on. Colonel William Drummond of the 104th (New Brunswick) Regiment, which had recently arrived at Kingston after an overland winter march and whose companies were in the vanguard of the attack along with Newfoundland "marines," strode up to Prevost and said, "Allow me a few minutes sir, and I will put you in possession of the place." Prevost curtly rebuffed him with, "Obey your orders sir, and learn the first duties of a soldier."[7]

Instead of pressing his advantage, Prevost chose to retreat to his ships and return home to Kingston. The battle of Sackett's Harbour gained little for the British tactically but did much to shake the confidence of their field commanders in their commander-in-chief. The only damage Prevost had done was to lose 260 of his men. The Americans did the real damage to their own facilities. To the Royal Newfoundland Regiment it meant another hard fought fight and another long casualty list. Once again they were commended by Adjutant General Baynes who noted that, "The detachment of the Royal Newfoundland Regiment behaved with great gallantry." Their casualty list read four killed, thirteen wounded and one missing.[8]

Brigadier General Vincent meanwhile, had moved on to a place called 40 Mile Creek where he paused for two days to take stock of his situation and finalize his plan of retreat. He had lost 458 men in the defence of Fort George. The Royal Newfoundland Regiment had again suffered heavily. Both Captain Winter and Lt. Stewart had been wounded as well as ten others, five of whom were captured. Twenty-one of the Newfoundland grenadiers had paid the supreme sacrifice.[9]

Vincent planned to retreat along the ridge of the south shore of Lake Ontario to its head and the height of land there called Burlington Heights. There, with the lake at his back he could command all the surrounding countryside. He could also open up a line of communication with Procter at Fort Amherstburg while ensuring Procter of keeping his supply lines open to Kingston.

The Americans were slow to follow Vincent and it was not until June 5th, four days after the fleeing British had reached and established a camp at Burlington Heights consisting of a crude fortification of piled logs and earthenworks, that Generals Winder and Chandler with a force of infantry, cavalry and artillery numbering 2,000 men reached Stoney Creek about seven miles below Vincent's position.

There the Americans ran into Vincent's Newfoundland and Glengarry pickets who after a brief skirmish retreated to Burlington Heights. The Americans halted and threw up a hasty camp. The Americans did not expect to be attacked by a force which they believed to be less than half their size and which was already in retreat. They set up their camp haphazardly, stringing their tents loosely and placing their artillery carelessly. A British scouting party reported that the camp was badly set up and surprise attack could easily rout it.

Colonel John Harvey, commanding the 49th, suggested a night attack to Vincent, confident that a hand picked force could surprise and capture the American camp. Vincent, unlike his commander Prevost, listened to his field officer.

Harvey asked for 700 hand picked volunteers from the command and also volunteered to personally lead them. Since the British were down to ninety rounds of ammunition per man, Harvey proposed to take the outlying posts silently and once into the main camp strike with a quick bayonet charge.[10]

He hand picked 704 men from all the Corps that were gathered at Burlington Heights—the 49th, 41st, 8th and 104th Regiments of Foot, and the Newfoundlanders and Glengarries. The bulk of the Newfoundland Regiment was posted to repel any attack that might come from American boats moving up the lake shore. As Vincent reported, "...the Newfoundland under Lt. Col. Bisshopp was confided, during the absence of the other troops, the important task of the defence of this extensive position."[11]

The British left for the attack from Burlington Heights early on the evening of July 5th, and made their way silently and stealthily to the American camp on Stoney Creek. About midnight they reached the Bluecoat lines and Harvey dispersed his "commandos" into small groups to bayonet the outlying sentries and pickets. This was quietly and efficiently done as Harvey reported, "In conformity with directions I had given, the sentries at the outskirts of the enemy's camp were bayoneted in the quickest manner and the camp immediately stormed."[12]

Just as Harvey was closing on the main camp he lost some of the advantage of his silent attack. Horses began to spook and sentries began to shout to comrades who could not answer. FitzGibbon with the 49th, ordered his men to charge with levelled bayonets. The Americans, initially surprised, quickly regrouped and began a cutting fire of musketry. The British were dispersed but quickly regrouped and made another lightning bayonet charge, breaking through the American line and scattering the Bluecoats in confusion. A contingent of the 49th charged the battery, driving off its defenders and captured two of the guns.

In the confused melee, General Winder found himself surrounded by shouting and charging men which he tried to rally in the darkness only to find that they were British soldiers and not his own. Winder was quickly taken prisoner, as was General Chandler who was wounded in the capture of the American gun battery. Without their commanders, the Americans broke and retreated, leaving their tents, provisions and their dead on the battlefield.[13]

Col. Harvey quickly reported to General Vincent and awaited further orders. Stoney Creek was in British hands but they had suffered more serious losses than the Americans. The Bluecoats had only lost 180 men while the British suffered 216 casualties. Harvey's force of now less than 500 could face a counter-attack by a force that still numbered almost six times that. Accordingly, Vincent ordered Harvey to withdraw to Burlington Heights with his spoils and provisions, fearful that the Americans would learn the actual strength of his forces and mount a concerted attack on his position. Harvey took what provisions and ammunition he could carry, as well as two of the American guns, and with 125 American prisoners, including the two U.S. Generals and five other field officers, he withdrew to Vincent's headquarters.

The fleeing Americans did not stop until they reached 40 Mile Creek where they awaited further orders, or at least a field officer to give them some. While they waited a new threat appeared. Sir James Yeo of the Royal Navy and his fleet of six ships had recently been to Vincent's headquarters at Burlington Heights where he had delivered supplies and 100 reinforcements and was now coasting down the lake to Kingston when he spotted the American camp at 40 Mile

Creek. Yeo, as was custom, sent for the surrender of the camp, which, as was custom, was politely refused. Yeo bombarded the camp with his cannon then sent his Newfoundland "marines" ashore to assault it.

The reluctant American commander, Colonel James Burn of the 2nd Light Dragoons believed that Yeo's ships carried a large force of British troops and quickly retired to Fort George. Yeo then returned to Burlington Heights and took on board the 180 American prisoners for transport to Montreal. He landed them at York from where they were marched overland to Montreal under a guard of the Royal Newfoundland Regiment. Major General de Rottenburg wrote Adjutant General Baynes from 12 Mile Creek that, "The light company of the Newfoundland Regiment left York long ago as an escort to the prisoners taken at Stoney Creek, and I trust ere this they have arrived at Kingston."[14]

Following the encounter at 40 Mile Creek, the Americans convinced the British were mounting a massive counter-attack, retreated from all their captured position on the Niagara River to Fort George. General Vincent, surprised at this lucky change of fortunes was not foolhardy enough to go chasing after them. He knew his forces were still outnumbered by more than two to one. As he appraised his situation he was in communication with Brig. Gen. Procter at Fort Amherstburg who had been constantly petitioning Governor Prevost for more men and supplies. Adj. Gen. Baynes at Kingston told Procter that Vincent meant to take a stand at Burlington Heights but in the event that he was forced to retreat to Kingston, he had directed Vincent "to detach to your (Gen. Procter) assistance the remainder of the three companies of the Newfoundland and Glengarry Regiments; the companies of the two latter Corps. are much weakened by the action of the 27th."[15]

General Vincent was not as confident as Baynes about his position. He also protested sending Procter any more men, but not because he couldn't spare them. He felt, like Procter, that the high command in Montreal had not been doing enough to support the Detroit frontier, and that sending Procter more men without ensuring his supply lines would "add to Brig. Gen. Procter's misery in sending him the remaining companies of the...Newfoundland and part of the Glengarry."[16]

But as summer wore on and the Americans made no attempt to attack Burlington Heights, Vincent relaxed a little as he prepared for an offensive on Fort George. With the supply routes to Fort Amherstburg secure he sent the remaining, diminished company of the Royal Newfoundland Regiment consisting of fifty-eight men under Captain Whalen west to Fort Amherstburg to reinforce Procter's undermanned command.

PROFILE; LAURA SECORD "HEROINE OF CANADA"

The Battle of Beaver Dams, fought between 570 American regulars and mounted frontiersmen, and a company of less than fifty British regulars and 400 Caughnawaga and Mohawk Indians on June 24, 1813, is considered one of the pivotal points of the conflict on the Niagara Frontier which gave the British the offensive. Although there was great loss of life, the battle is not considered to be one of the major engagements of the war. Yet it is fraught with myth and mystery, icons and irony, and if not magic, then certainly blind luck.

On the evening of June 23rd, a handful of American Army officers stopped at the Secord Inn in Queenston on the Niagara River to take their supper. As they dined, they were overheard by a "slight, delicate little Loyalist woman in a gingham dress"[17] discussing their plans to attack a British outpost near Beaver Dams, about twelve miles west of Queenston. The outpost was the front line headquarters of Lt. James FitzGibbon who with his small company of regulars and Indian guerillas had been harassing the advancing American lines on the Niagara frontier.

The "little loyalist woman" whose name was Laura (nee: Ingersoll) Secord decided to warn FitzGibbon and his men of the planned American attack. She was born on September 13, 1775 in Great Barrington, Massachusetts the daughter of a loyalist who waited twenty years before he took his family to the Niagara River where he opened an Inn at Queenston. A year later, young Laura married James Secord, a local merchant, who like his father-in-law was a patriot of England.[18] Secord had been at the Battle of Queenston Heights with General Isaac Brock the year before as a member of a local militia and had been severely wounded. He was still an invalid when his wife informed him of the Americans' plan. Since he could not hope to take the warning to FitzGibbon in time, Laura decided that she must go.

Far from being the "slight and delicate little loyalist woman in a gingham dress," Laura was by now thirty-eight years old and the mother of five children, inured to a hard and spartan frontier life. She had the year before gone to the killing field that was Queenston Heights to find her twice wounded husband who was bleeding to death and "shouldered him to their nearby home and slowly nursed him back to health."[19]

As evening of June 22nd was drawing on, she left Secord's Inn and, as myth would have us believe, leading a cow to an evening milking rushed her way through admiring American sentries. The cow did not exist, but there may be some truth to the speculation that she did carry a milking stool with her in her attempt to deceive the sentries.[20]

After walking all night and the whole of the next day, she finally reached Beaver Dams on the evening of June 23rd, after a gruelling walk of nineteen miles, in a circuitous route to avoid American sentries along the roads. Her trek took her through thick woods that offered the danger of encountering wildcats or poisonous snakes, and mosquito infested swamplands where a broiling sun beat down on her all day. A mile or so from her destination she stumbled into one of the camps of the Caughnawaga Indians, where for a few long minutes she feared for her life.

"The chief at first objected to letting me pass," she later recounted, "but finally consented, after some hesitation to go with me to FitzGibbon's station, which was at Beaver Dam, where I had an interview with him. I told him...that the Americans intended to make an attack upon the troops un-

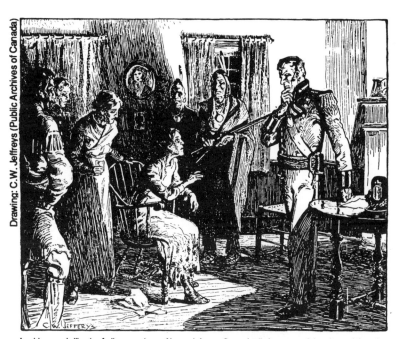

Looking much like the frail, young lass of legend, Laura Secord tells her story of the planned American attack on Beaver Dams to Capt. Fitzgibbon of the British 49th Regiment

der his command, and would from their superior numbers, capture them all."[21]

FitzGibbon listened to Mrs. Secord's story intently, assured her that he would act on her information, then had the woman ushered into the confines of his camp where she was fed and tended to. The frontier, FitzGibbon knew, was alive with spies, some burning both ends of the candle. He could not say how Laura Secord knew what she did, but he could say that it was true. What he also could not say was anything to Laura Secord. He already knew of the American plan from his Indian scouts and had positioned them where the woman had stumbled upon them in the woods to ambush the Americans as they marched on Beaver Dams.[22]

Just about dawn on June 24th, Lt. Col. Charles Boerstler, and his 750 troops, marched unknowingly into the waiting

trap of the British and their Indian allies a few miles east of
Beaver Dams. In a thickly wooded area of beach trees the
Indians ambushed the Americans forcing them to disperse
and seek cover in the woods. The Caughnawaga and Mohawks had laid their trap well and the Americans suffered
heavy casualties before they were able to dig in.

For three hours the Indians fought their kind of battle,
flittering through the woods in their paint and camouflage,
sniping at the American troops who were stationary and
confused. By late morning, Boerstler and his men were completely pinned down under a boiling sun and nearly out of
ammunition. They had already suffered 200 casualties and
the Indians were preparing to move in with the tomahawk
and the scalping knife.

By now Lt. FitzGibbon was on the scene, but he realized
that with his company of less than fifty men he could not
force the Americans to surrender. He was anxiously awaiting
reinforcement from 12 Mile Creek to the west of him, but at
the same time knew that the Indians, once they were sure the
Americans were out of ammunition, would move in for a
massacre and scalp-hunt. FitzGibbon, who had tried a brazen bluff on the Americans at Stoney Creek only a few weeks
earlier, decided to run another one.

He raised a flag of truce and went out to meet the American officers. He told Boerstler that he was in advance of a
large force that had the Americans completely surrounded
and further fighting would be senseless. The American commander demanded to see his men, commenting that he was
"not accustomed to surrender to an army he has not seen."
FitzGibbon knew his hand had been called and frantically
searched for a way not to have to show it. Luckily, a small
detachment of Provincial Dragoons arrived on the scene and

the Lt. convinced its Captain to act as the officer in charge of the large force which had the Americans surrounded.

Boerstler, still not convinced, asked for time to consider. FitzGibbon continued to press him, playing for time, and cautioning that he could not control the Indians much longer. His delaying tactics and veiled threats of an Indian massacre bought him the time that he needed. Soon his commander, Major DeHaren did arrive on the scene, but he too did not have enough men to force the Americans to surrender. FitzGibbon, with a lot of fast talk and fancy footwork also manipulated the unknowing Major into going along with his dangerous charade. As the American troops began to march towards the greatly outnumbered British lines, the nervy Lieutenant tried one more bluff to get them to lay down their muskets. He said that for the American troops to march still armed into the British ranks through the Indians would cause the Indians to react with hostility.

The American commander, remembering Frenchtown and the Raisin River implored FitzGibbon, "For God's sake, keep the Indians from us!"[23] Boerstler had his men lay down their muskets. FitzGibbon had them. He had run the gauntlet of his bluff and had won.

FitzGibbon's warnings about not being able to control his Indians proved to be only half fallacy. The warriors quickly swarmed into the American ranks, plundering muskets, swords and ammunition, and brandishing their tomahawks and scalping knives at the now disarmed prisoners. The Lieutenant quickly took charge, warning the Indians off and reminding their chiefs that they had given their word no prisoners would be harmed. The Caughnawaga chiefs kept their word and controlled their braves, but showed that they were more than a little displeased with the outcome of the battle.

The Caughnawaga, who had lost fifteen of their warriors killed and twenty-five wounded, were now denied the battle honour of scalping the dead. The Mohawks, who had taken little part in the battle got most of the plunder, and the British army got all the glory. As one Mohawk chief later put it, "The Caughnawaga Indians fought the battle, the Mohawks got the plunder and FitzGibbon got the credit."[24]

As for Laura Secord, the "heroine" of the Beaver Dams, history is still bemused. The romantic picture of the young, wispy, comely maiden, thrashing for almost twenty miles through woods and swamps to warn the British that the "Americans are coming!" is a stirring vision and the stuff that myths are made of. Her gruelling trek, whatever the reason undertaken, is in itself a testimony to the courage, stamina and perseverance of a hardy frontier woman, who like many others of her time, saw a duty and did it. Even though her journey was unnecessary she could not have known that, and the fortitude she showed in undertaking it is in itself commendable and worthy of commemoration.[25]

But forgotten in the "myth" are the real heroes of the Battle of Beaver Dams, the Caughnawaga Indians, and a brazen Lieutenant of the regular British Army, who although taking many lives, also probably saved many more.

Endnotes:

1. Stanley; op. cit., p. 180.
2. Berton; op. cit., p. 68.
3. Saunders; op. cit., p. 37.
4. Ibid.
5. Nicholson; op. cit., p. 77.
6. Raddall; op. cit., p. 146.
7. Saunders; op. cit., p. 31. After Prevost withdrew to his Royal Navy ships, one of his Colonels was heard to comment as he climbed back aboard one of the ships, "If he would but give me my own regiment, I would land again, and have the place." Many of Prevost's officers were critical of his field tactics; some even believed he was cowardly. He was not willing to go on with the attack even though his officers, such as Col. Drummond, who led the 104th New Brunswick was, even though Drummond's Regiment had suffered the heaviest losses of the attack. The New Brunswick Regiment suffered 78 casualties of the 261, the heaviest of any of the Corps involved in the action at Sackett's Harbour.
8. Ibid., p. 34. After the war Prevost was brought up on charges and court-martialled for his action at Sackett's Harbour. However, he died in England in 1815 before his trial began. Posthumously, he was spoken of politely, but some of the officers who had been with him believed that he was at least guilty of negligence if not outright cowardice.
9. Nicholson; p. 77.
10. Cochrane; Hugh F.; "Tiger in the Forest: Fitzgibbon of the 49th." *Canadian Frontier: 1976.* p. 7.
    One of the most brazen, and lucky "scouts" of the British reconnaissance of the evening of June 5th, was Lt. James Fitzgibbon of the 49th (Royal Irish) Regiment. He dressed as a farmer and with a basketful of butter wandered unchallenged into the American lines pretending to be looking for a sale for his wares. He wandered the whole encampment learning the positions of sentries and guards, and the location of troops and artillery. At one point he was challenged by an American officer who questioned him about British troop movements but Fitzgibbon carried off his role as the ignorant, simple farmer well and returned to Burlington Heights with the information that convinced General Vincent to make a night attack on Stoney Creek.
11. Saunders; op. cit., p. 23.
12. Ibid., p. 24.
13. Stanley; op. cit., p. 188. General Winder, who when he discovered he was surrounded by British troops was about to offer his pistol in surrender when Sgt. Alexander Fraser of the 49th levelled his bayoneted musket at the American officer and cautioned, "If you stir, Sir, you die." Winder dropped his pistol and sword and replied, "I am your prisoner." Unknown to Winder, his slightest move probably would have cost him his life. Sgt. Fraser had bayoneted seven American sentries that night and his younger brother who stood beside him had bayoneted four.
14. Saunders; op. cit., p. 25.
15. Ibid., p. 38.
16. Ibid., p. 25.
17. Berton, Pierre; *Flames Across The Border.* p. 83.
18. Whalen, Dwight; "Laura Secord: Heroine of Upper Canada," *Canadian Frontier:* Vol. 2., No. 3, 1973, p. 31.

19. See endnote number 2.
20. Raddall; op. cit., p. 248.
21. Whalen; op. cit., p. 32.
22. Raddall; op. cit., p. 249.
23. Berton; op. cit., p. 89.
24. See endnote number 7, p. 91.
25. Whalen; op. cit., p. 33. Throughout her long life—Laura Secord died at the age of ninety-three on October 17, 1868—she never revealed to any living person, as far as can be determined, where or from whom she received the information of the impending American attack on Beaver Dams. Even the American commander, Lt. Col. Boerstler, did not know that he was to march on Beaver Dams until June 23rd. Laura Secord had left with the news of the attack on the evening of June 22nd. Such is the stuff of legends and myths.

CHAPTER NINE

Royal Newfoundland "Marines"

HILE THE BRITISH prepared for a counter-attack on the Niagara frontier, Brigadier-General Procter planned to mount his own offensive on the Detroit frontier. Although he still had control of Lake Erie, he knew that the Americans were busy building a "fleet" at Presque Isle on the southern shore of the lake, much in the same way that they had at Sackett's Harbour on Lake Ontario. Too, he knew that Harrisson's forces were being reinforced by hundreds of men as each week of the early summer went by. Still without any real support, or even direction from the high command in the east, he decided he had to move before the enemy became too strong for him to defeat.

By now Procter had almost given up on the idea of trying to capture Fort Meigs; it had been too strong for him in April and it was probably even stronger now. Besides all the other pressures on him he also had to contend with Tecumseh and his Indian warriors who were getting restless and demanding their Redcoat brothers lead them in another attack against the Bluecoats. Tecumseh told Procter that his warriors were losing confidence in his leadership and if he did not do something he could not guarantee that his Indians would remain in his ranks.

Procter asked the Shawnee chief's advice. Tecumseh pro-

posed a plan for a second attack on Fort Meigs which the
British commander reluctantly agreed with. In late July,
Procter left Fort Amherstburg with 1,500 men; 400 regulars
— including the two companies of the Royal Newfoundland
Regiment under Captain Mockler and Whelan — 100 militiamen, and about 1,000 Indians, for Fort Meigs on the Maumee
River. Tecumseh's plan was to stage a mock battle in the
woods near the American fort in hopes it would make the
enemy believe a relief column was being attacked and spur
them to come to its rescue. The Indians and British would
then ambush them, rush the fort and capture it. The plan was
a simple one and might have worked except that the fort's
commander, Gen. Clay had learned earlier that day that
Procter's force was near and he himself was not expecting
any relief or supply columns. The ruse did not work. The
Americans didn't budge from their fort.[1]

The next day it rained incessantly and most of the Indians, discouraged, drifted off home. Some remained with
Tecumseh and Procter who now decided that if he was to
keep his Indian allies he must give them a victory. He set his
sights on the small post of Fort Stephenson on the Sandusky
River about twenty miles east of Fort Meigs. The American
post was a crude frontier fortification, protected by a ditch, a
log palisade and one 6-pounder cannon. It was manned by
160 men under the command of Major George Croghan.
Here, Procter believed, he could win a small victory which
would regain the confidence of his Indian allies.

Procter arrived at Fort Stephenson on August 1st and
sent the customary invitation to surrender to Major Croghan,
which, as usual, was customarily refused. He brought up his
cannon and fired several rounds at the fort but the light guns
had little effect on the thick log walls. The next day, Tecumseh's Indians began to complain even more about the compe-

tence of their British allies. Many of them began to drift home to their villages. Procter was eventually convinced by the Indian agents who had accompanied him that if he was to save face with the Indians he must make a charge against the fort.

Procter was not prepared for such a charge. His light guns could not punch a hole in the palisades, he had no scaling ladders to climb the walls, and the few axes his men had were too blunt to chop through the thick walls of the fort. Yet attack he did, and when his men reached the ditch surrounding the stockade they found one more staunch surprise from the seemingly defenceless fort.

The "ditch" surrounding the post proved to be a pitfall, being twelve feet wide and eight feet deep, the palisades towering above another ten feet. As the British troops tried to scramble up the slippery sides of the ditch and hack at the thick log walls, the Americans picked them off from their musket loopholes and raked them with grapeshot along the line of the ditch with their one 6-pounder cannon.

Within a few minutes nearly 100 of the British attackers lay déad or wounded in the ditch. The others managed to retreat with most of the wounded but nineteen were abandoned in the dry moat. During the night the Indians managed to rescue them and by morning Procter and his troops had boarded their boats for Amherstburg and Tecumseh's Indians had struck out overland to return to their villages.[2]

Procter's desperate attempt to inflict a damaging blow on the converging Americans on the Detroit frontier went unnoticed by the enemy. They were biding their time and building their forces. The British commander knew he was soon to face a huge American assault and he also knew that neither he nor the Royal Navy on Lake Erie were ready for it.

By August of 1813, Procter was petitioning Governor

Prevost increasingly for more men to man the Royal Navy ships on Lake Erie so that he could make a pre-emptive strike against the American shipyard at Presque Isle, and then mount concerted attacks on General Harrisson's forces at Fort Meigs and Fort Stephenson. The Governor promised more but was very slow in delivering, and when he did it was very little. By late August the Americans had completed the shipbuilding and were conducting an increasingly successful blockade of the British supply routes from Kingston to Fort Amherstburg.

Command of the Royal Navy "fleet" on Lake Erie was in the hands of Captain Robert H. Barclay, a young career officer thirty-two years old who had seen action at Trafalger with Nelson and had lost an arm in the battle. He told Procter that his ships were already undermanned even for the transport duty he was performing, and if he had to do battle with the Americans he would need at least 300 additional seamen. Procter forwarded Barclay's request for the sailors, emphasizing that, "There are not in the fleet more than four and twenty seamen."[3]

Capt. Barclay specifically requested members of the Royal Newfoundland Regiment for his crews. As he wrote Prevost, it was his "strong desire to have some more of the R.N. Fland Regt. as his greatest reliance is on those of that Corps at present employed as Marines."[4] Strong desire or not, Barclay was not to get them. By the end of the month he decided he could wait no longer. He had to strike first.

In desperation, Procter gathered every man he could spare from Fort Amherstburg and assigned them duty aboard Barclay's ships. They included fifty-eight men of Capt. Whelan's Newfoundland company which now brought the total number of the Regiment serving in the "marines" on the lake to just over 100. The General also put

150 men of the 41st Regiment on board the ships but this still left Barclay fifty men short of his full crew complements. Procter explained to Barclay that this was the best he could do, commenting as the men of the 41st Regiment boarded the ships, "Better soldiers there cannot be, but they are only landsmen.[5]

Barclay did receive some help from Yeo however, when on September 5th, of the 300 seamen he had requested thirty-eight arrived from Kingston. Barclay was disgusted and said so to his superior. "The number," he wrote Yeo, "is totally inadequate to render the squadron under my command effective."[6] But ready or not Barclay found he had to fight.

On the evening of Sept. 9, 1813, Commodore Barclay set sail from the Detroit River for Put-in-Bay at the mouth of the Sandusky River on the south shore of Lake Erie. He had with him six ships: his flagship the *Detroit*, the *Queen Charlotte*, the *Lady Prevost*, the *Hunter*, the *Chippewa*, and the *Little Belt*. His ships were armed with sixty-five guns, many of which were long range cannon and would be of little use in close-up combat. His crews amounted to 407 officers and men, including the fifty-five Royal Navy sailors, the 100 Canadian Provincial Marine seamen, the 150 soldiers of the 41st Regiment and just over 100 of the Royal Newfoundland Regiment who again had been assigned duties as sailors, gunners, and marines.[7]

Shortly after sunrise on the following morning as he approached Put-in-Bay, the Americans came out to meet Barclay's fleet. Their commander was Captain Oliver H. Perry, whose fleet totalled nine ships: Perry's flagship the *Lawrence*, the *Niagara*, the *Caledonia*, the *Tigress*, the *Ariel*, the *Scorpion*, and the *Somers*, the *Porcupine*, and the *Trippe*. His ships carried only fifty-five guns, but most of them were lighter cannon which were better for close-in battle. His crews numbered 532 officers and men, about sixty percent of whom were experienced seamen from the Atlantic coast. The others were Kentucky riflemen he had boarded to use as "sharpshooters."

The two fleets drew within range of each other shortly before noon off West Sister Island in Put-in-Bay and the Battle of Lake Erie was on.

Seeing he was outnumbered, Barclay immediately pressed the attack, bringing his long range guns into full action, hoping to gain a quick advantage. He did initially, for as the ships closed range his long guns pounded Perry's flagship *Lawrence* and by the time it was in range it had been so badly damaged by Barclay's fire that Perry was forced to strike his colours and board his second ship-of-the-line, the *Niagara* to continue the battle from her decks. Barclay's flag-ship *Detroit*, was also badly battered but still able to fight on.[8]

Commander Barclay however, was not. He was badly wounded by flying wood and his first Lieutenant was killed. Command of the ship fell to a less experienced Lieutenant who when he saw Perry abandon the *Lawrence* prepared to board the American ship and take it prisoner. As he went to load his boarding party he found that all his ship's boats were smashed and in the meantime the *Detroit* had become a sitting duck in the water as the other American vessels closed in on her.

The *Queen Charlotte*, the second largest ship in the British fleet could not come to the *Detroit's* aid as it was also badly damaged and both its Captain and first Lieutenant had been killed.

Aboard the *Niagara*, which had taken little part in the initial engagement and suffered no damage in the by now two hour old battle, Commodore Perry raised his colours and moved in for the kill. As he closed, the *Detroit* and *Queen*

Charlotte attempted to manoeuvre to meet him, but in the becalming winds the two British ships tangled their bowsprits and could not free themselves. Perry turned his vessel broadside and blasted both British ships with cannonballs and grapeshot while the Kentucky riflemen raked their decks with a deadly musket fire. Unable to free themselves, their cannons were of little use, the British officers decided to end the savage slaughter and struck their colours in surrender.

Perry now turned his attention to the *Hunter* and the *Lady Prevost*, which by now were badly shot up and faltering. Outnumbered four to one, the two British vessels were soon crippled and unable to fight or flee. They struck their colours and surrendered and upon seeing this the two smallest of the British ships, the *Chippewa* and the *Little Belt* turned sails to home. Perry's smaller, faster clipper gave chase and soon overtook them. The Battle of Lake Erie was over; the entire British fleet had been captured.

The hard fought, brutal battle had lasted for three hours and saw sixty-eight men lose their lives and 190 maimed and wounded. The British lost forty-one killed and ninety-four wounded; the Americans had twenty-seven killed and ninety-six wounded. Among the British dead were three officers, Barclay's first Lieutenant on board the *Detroit*, and the captain and first lieutenant of the *Queen Charlotte*, James Garden of the Royal Newfoundland Regiment, who was serving aboard the ship as gunnery Captain.

Lt. Garden and the two other British officers, along with three American officers also killed in the battle were a couple of days later buried with a full military honours funeral side by side on South Bass Island in Put-in-Bay.[9]

As well as Lt. Garden, fourteen other members of the Newfoundland Regiment were killed. They included six non-commissioned officers and eight rank and file. Their

Soldiers of the Royal Newfoundland Regiment served as "marines" and "seamen" on board Capt.
Barkley's ships at the Battle of Lake Erie, 1813. As Barkley later reported: "The gunners being without matches or tubes fit to fire, had to fire pistols at the priming (of the cannons) to set the guns off."

remains were committed to the deeps of Lake Erie even as the
battle raged. Once again the Newfoundlanders bore the
brunt of a savage battle and distinguished themselves with
honour. Of the 135 casualties the British suffered that day,
forty of them were from the Royal Newfoundland Regiment
— almost thirty percent of the total, even though they made
up only twenty-five percent of the total British force. The
remaining Newfoundlanders, twenty-five of whom were
badly wounded were forced on a gruelling march through
Ohio to Frankfort, Kentucky where they remained prisoners
of war until its end.[10]

Captain Barclay, once again maimed, was paroled
shortly after his capture. A one armed Captain who could
only use half of his remaining one was of little threat to the
American Navy. Barclay spoke glowingly of the conduct and
bravery of the men of the Newfoundland Regiment. "The

conduct of the soldiers serving on board as marines has excited my warmest thanks and admiration."[11] He put the blame on the defeat squarely on the shoulders of his superiors, Sir James Yeo, commanding the Royal Navy, and Sir George Prevost, commanding the British Army. In Barclay's opinion the one cause for his loss was their refusal to send him the experienced seamen he had begged them for all summer. As he put it, his defeat was due to "the lack of good seamen arriving in time from Newfoundland; the authorities not aware of the urgent need of them."[12] A year after the Battle of Lake Erie, the battered Barclay was court-martialled for the loss of his fleet on Lake Erie. The court however, found that he was not to blame and that all his officers and men had "conducted themselves in the most gallant manner."

The total annihilation of the British fleet on Lake Erie threw wide open the doors for an American attack on the British held Detroit front. General Procter and his command at Forts Ameherstburg and Detroit now faced the unbridled onslaught of Perry's navy and Harrisson's army. Procter had lost 250 more of his regular troops in the Lake Erie battle and had only about 750 regulars left to him that were fit for duty. One hundred were either too ill, or were still recovering from wounds, to be of use in battle.

He knew that he could not count on raising any great number of militia as harvest season was fast approaching. His greatest ally would be Tecumseh's Indians and the faithful, but by now tired, Shawnee chief rallied to his support with 1,200 warriors. But against Harrisson's massed forces of almost 5,000 and with Perry's ships in command of Lake Erie, Procter knew he had no change but to cut and run.

On September 18th, Procter ordered the captured Fort Detroit burned and his outpost there to cross the river and

The Royal Newfoundland Regiment made up thirty percent of the British forces which took part in the naval engagement that was the Battle of Lake Erie, fought on September 10, 1813.

join him at Amherstburg in preparation for a general retreat up the valley of the Thames River to Lake Ontario and the safety of British held territory. The proud Tecumseh expressed disdain at this move and openly taunted Procter, going so far as to call him a coward publicly. Procter was unperturbed by the Indian's belittling and went ahead with his plan for a full scale withdrawal of his forces from the Detroit frontier.[13]

A week later he gave orders to burn Fort Amherstburg and began his retreat northeastwards up the Thames River. General Harrisson was hot on his heels and soon caught up to Procter's slow moving caravan, struggling through the muddy, autumn soaked roads with its burden of wounded and sick, and women and children. At a small village called Moraviantown on the Thames, Harrisson's army caught up to Procter's pitiful retreat column on October 5th, and prepared to do battle.

Procter was not prepared to surrender and neither was Tecumseh. The Shawnee chief had earlier, prophetically, predicted that this would be his last stand. In the battle that later followed—if it could be called a battle—the Indian chief and his warriors took the brunt of the American attack, allowing Procter and some of his men time to evacuate the civilians to safety. Tecumseh was cut down in a dragoon charge and Procter lost twelve men killed, thirty-six wounded and 477 taken prisoner by the swift attack of Harrisson's cavalry. Besides Tecumseh the Indians lost thirty-three killed. The Kentucky riflemen were not known for taking Indian prisoners.[14]

The British commander halted his retreat at Ancaster, not far from Gen. Vincent's flanks at Burlington Heights. From there, Procter tried to learn the fate of his 477 men taken prisoner, virtually his entire command. He sent Lt. LeBreton of the Royal Newfoundland Regiment as his emissary to Harrisson who had given up his pursuit and returned to Detroit to consolidate his newly captured territory.

Harrisson was in no mood to entertain the queries of the British, and even less prepared to advise them of the disposition of the prisoners he had taken. Lt. LeBreton became a "hostage" for several weeks as Harrisson hurried his preparations to remove British prisoners from the front. The war was becoming more and more brutal and both sides no longer found themselves willing to readily exchange prisoners which they knew might well return to fight them another day.

Dispatches from Procter and Vincent to learn the whereabouts of LeBreton were politely, but tardily responded to by Harrisson who wrote Gen. Vincent in late October, "Lieut.

The Death of Tecumseh at the "Battle of the Thames" October, 1813

LeBreton, an officer in your service, arrived at Detroit...bearing a flag and a letter to me from Gen. Procter, requesting humane treatment for the prisoners in my possession...With respect to the subject of Gen. Procter's letter, those which I have to enclose you from the British officers who were taken on the fifth...to their families, and the report of Mr. LeBreton will satisfy you that no indulgence which humanity can claim in their favour, or the usages of war sanction has been withheld..."[15]

The British prisoners in Harrisson's custody were soon to learn more about the "usages of war" than they were about the "indulgence of humanity." Procter's 477 prisoners were sent to Ohio, where at "Camp Bull, outside Chillicothe, there were fifty-nine men and officers of the Royal Newfoundland Regiment within its walls." These were the men of Barclay's fleet who had been taken in the Battle of Lake Erie and had been held since then as one observer wrote, "confined in jail and handcuffed and subjected to considerable indignities." From Camp Bull, the Newfoundlanders and their comrades were ferried to the Kentucky River then marched overland to prison at Frankfort, Kentucky.[16]

The Detroit frontier was lost to the British, but not by lack of effort on the part of Procter and his besieged Corps which included companies of the Royal Newfoundland Regiment. As one observer wrote, "For more than fourteen months the little British army on the Detroit, thousands of miles from home, had marched and fought in the wilderness against crazy odds, and in every extreme of weather. In that time, with the variable aid of the Indians, they had killed, wounded or captured more than four thousand Americans, mostly on American soil, and by all these exertions staved off the invasion of Canada from the West. It was a sorry end to a brave campaign.[17]

Drawing: C.W. Jeffreys (Public Archives of Canada)

Tecumseh meets General Brock: The night before Brock's attack on Fort Detroit, the Shawnee chief sat by late into the night as the General and his officers debated whether or not to attack. When Brock finally ended the debate at about 4:00 a.m. by declaring that he would attack, Tecumseh pointed to the General and said to his fellow chiefs, "Ho! This is a man."

PROFILE; Tecumseh: Redcoat Indian Ally

Tecumseh — (or Tecumtha or Tecumsée) was probably the most famous and successful Indian chief in northeastern North America in the latter years of the eighteenth, and the early years of the nineteenth centuries. Not since the great chief Pontiac, almost a half century before him were the Indians of the northeast so united in their attempts to resist the expansion of the white men and keep their hereditary lands for themselves. He was a statesman, a warrior, a leader and a visionary. Known to the white men as the "Red Bonaparte" for his skill in battle, he was known to his own people as a "prophet," who foresaw the day when all Indian tribes would stand together as one people in a free Indian Nation.

Tecumseh was a Shawnee Indian born in March, 1763 in the village of Piqua on the Mad River in what is today Ohio.[18] His name in his native tongue meant "Flying or Springing Across" and later became corrupted in English to "Panther" or "Shooting Star." He was born into a war clan of his tribe and grew up to be seasoned in that art. While still a boy of ten he was to learn his first real lessons in warfare which throughout his lifetime would be with the white men.

By this time, American settlers were beginning to intrude on Shawnee lands and clashes between the Indian and settlers resulted in bloody attacks and counter-attacks. With the outbreak of the American Revolution the Shawnee allied themselves with the British against the American enemy in the hope that a British victory would give them a guarantee that they would be left alone on their lands in the Ohio country.

When the Americans won the Revolutionary War, the Shawnee found themselves without their British allies and the Americans even more determined than before to settle on their lands. The long, bloody war had also instilled deep hatred of one another into both red and white hearts.

Most of the Shawnee's elders and leaders had either been killed or were too infirm to lead the young warriors in the resistance needed to defeat the Americans and drive them from Shawnee lands. Onto the stage stepped the young "Panther" or "Shooting Star," who was by now recognized among his people as a great warrior and champion of the Indian cause. He had been fighting the Americans both on the battlefield and in the Shawnee council houses since the American Revolution.

His vision was of one united Indian nation, encompassing all of the Indian tribes of eastern America who would establish a country of Indians for Indians, and free of white men. He worked tirelessly, almost fanatically to get the individual tribes to lay down their own hereditary feuds and differences and take up a common cause against the expansionist whites.

Tecumseh succeeded in bringing about a loose confederacy of the northeastern tribes from Ohio to the Missouri, bringing together such tribes as the Shawnee, Delaware, Kickapoo, Miami, Illinois, Winnebago, Monominee, Potawatami, and others. By 1810 he had forged the loose confederacy he had worked so long and hard for and was feared, and even respected by the expanding Americans.

He next turned his attention to the southern tribes and took long trips throughout the south, inciting tribes of the Creek, Choctaw, Chickasaw and Cherokee. He became almost fanatical in his message, cajoling and wooing the tribes with his great oratory. In his efforts he was not above preaching gloom and doom to those who would not follow him, even to the point of using veiled threats of divine retribution if his words were snubbed.

At a meeting with the Creek tribe at one of their main villages called Tukabatchi, after a long speech designed to recruit the Creeks into his fold, he suspected that their chief although seemingly receptive of his plea, really intended not to join him. "I leave Tukabatchi directly," Tecumseh told the chief, "and shall go to Detroit. When I arrive there, I will stamp my foot on the ground, and shake down every house in Tukabatchi."[19] Shortly after Tecumseh's departure the great earthquake of Madrid shook the southeastern U.S., and tumbled every house in the village of Tukabatchi to the ground. The terrified Creek Indians declared, "Tecumseh has got to Detroit!"

Among the Indian tribes, Tecumseh's fame now spread as a great prophet who spoke with the "great spirit." Tribe after tribe began to rally to his call and just as his complete confederacy seemed close to being realized disaster struck. At Tippecanoe Creek in Ohio country, an American force of 900 under command of General William Henry Harrisson raided Prophet's Town, which Tecumseh had set up as his "capital" of Indian territory. He had left the "town" under the charge of his brother, Tenskwata, who was known to the Indians as the "Prophet" and was believed by them to have magical powers and the gift of prophecy.

When Harrisson's men approached the Indian village, the "Prophet" told them that his magical powers would make them bulletproof and that they should attack. The Indians attacked at night but their greatest surprise proved to be that they were not bulletproof. They lost more than sixty of their warriors before they retreated far into the forest, abandoning Prophet's Town. Harrisson found the abandoned village the next day and burned it to the ground.[20]

When Tecumseh returned to find Prophet's Town destroyed early in 1812 he was infuriated with his brother, the

"Prophet" and threatened to kill him. With his foolish promise of "magic," Tenskwata had undone all Tecumseh had worked so hard to accomplish in the last ten years. The "Panther" had no choice but to move northward and seek an alliance with the British against his old enemies. When the War of 1812 broke out in June of that year, the Shawnee chief eagerly offered the service of his Indian confederacy to the "great white father."

The British eagerly accepted his offer and gave him a commission as a Brigadier General in the regular army. The Shawnee chief was quickly recognized as the undisputed leader of the Indian confederacy and Tecumseh was given independent command of the 2000 warriors who volunteered their services. It was now that the "Panther" would earn himself the moniker of the white men as the "Red Bonaparte."

In August he led 600 of his warriors on the attack on Detroit with Gen. Isaac Brock which saw Tecumseh lead only 600 warriors whom he made appear to be 5,000 to the hesitant commander of the American fort. The Americans raised the white flag and Detroit fell to the British virtually without a shot being fired. From Detroit, Tecumseh led his warriors on raiding parties, capturing and destroying several American outposts and striking terror into the hearts of his enemies.

In April of 1813, the Shawnee chief learned that his hated enemy, Gen. Harrisson had arrived on the Maumee River and built a fort from which he planned to attack the British Fort Amherstburg. Anxious to engage his old enemy, he gathered as many warriors as he could find and urged Gen. Procter to attack Harrisson's Fort Meigs. The attack turned into an unsuccessful siege and Tecumseh's faith in his British allies was shaken. When the British were defeated in the naval battle on Lake Erie later that summer, Gen. Procter decided to abandon his position and retreat to Lake Ontario. The "Red Bonaparte" was disgusted and accused his British ally of cowardice. In a rage, he shouted at Procter, "Begone! You are unfit to command: go and put on petticoats!"[21]

Tecumseh, however, was determined not to retreat. He longed for one last chance to kill his old enemy, Harrisson. As the burdened British caravan retreated, the "Panther" and his warriors hung back and engaged them in battle at Moraviantown on the Thames River on October 5, 1813. His warriors by now numbered only 500, many having deserted what they believed would be another lost cause. Tecumseh, also thought so, and shortly before the battle was said to have predicted his death.

With his 500 warriors he faced a force of 5,000, many of them cavalry. Tecumseh and his warriors fought valiantly but the Kentucky horsemen under Col. Richard Johnson continued to charge. The "Panther" rallied his warriors and charged into the ranks of the horsemen where he was shot in the chest and fell dead.

Tecumseh's death also meant the death of his dream. Without his leadership the grand plan of a great Indian confederacy also died. Some of the tribes continued to support the British throughout the war but others signed treaties with the Americans or switched allegiance. Never again would "the Indians of the Old Northwest approach the degree of unity that they had seen at the height of their success" under the "Red Bonaparte" of America.[22]

Endnotes:

1. Stanley; op. cit., p. 158.
2. Raddall; op. cit., p. 220.
3. Nicholson; op. cit., p. 78. Barclay had problems with his commander, Yeo, also. When he had arrived to take up his post on Lake Erie he complained that Yeo had supplied him with only six officers and "19 of the worst men in his squadron."
4. Ibid.
5. Ibid.
6. Saunders; op. cit., p. 12.
7. Raddall; p. 226-227.
8. Berton; *Flames Across The Border*, p. 166.
9. Nicholson; op. cit., p. 81. In 1913 an "imposing monument was erected over the remains to commemorate the battle and to serve as a permanent International Peace Memorial."
10. Ibid.
11. Saunders; op. cit., p. 13.
12. Ibid, p. 9.
13. Stanley; op. cit., p. 206.
14. Raddall; op. cit., p. 238.
15. Saunders; op. cit., p. 51.
16. Ibid., p. 52.
17. Raddall; op. cit., p. 237.
18. Bronson, L.N.; "The Search for Tecumseh." *Canadian Frontier*. Vol. 3, No. 1. 1974, p. 14.
19. Hook, Jason; *American Indian Warrior Chiefs*, p. 32.
20. Every, Dale Van; *The Final Challenge*, p. 113.
21. Hook; op. cit., p. 38.
22. Dwod, Gregory Evans; *A Spirited Resistance*, p. 185.

CHAPTER TEN

The "Mississippi Volunteers"

ITH THE LOSS OF THE DETROIT FRONTIER, and having only a tenuous foothold on the Niagara, the British began to brace themselves for the "real" invasion of Canada. They had, like the Americans had intended, been fighting a flank action in Upper Canada—the Americans real aim was Lower Canada and its capital of Quebec city. Now, with Lake Erie firmly on their hands, and Lake Ontario merely a thorn in their side, they could begin the real campaign to take the Canadas. First, they would take Montreal and the Upper St. Lawrence River, then descend the waterway to Quebec and the seat of the British colonial government.

By the end of October, 1813, the Americans had amassed an army of 8,000 men, fifty-eight field guns and a fleet of 300 boats under General James Wilkinson at the head of the St. Lawrence River, his rear protected by Commodore Chauncey's American fleet on the lake, to be joined by another American force striking up the St. Lawrence from Lake Champlain and the Richilieu River and attack and capture Montreal. There, the Americans would consolidate and reinforce then strike down the St. Lawrence to capture Quebec city.[1]

Within a few days, Wilkinson had begun moving his men

and equipment in his boats down the St. Lawrence River. Commander Yeo, and his British fleet, did not challenge Commodore Chauncey but small, fast gunboats from Kingston, commanded by Captain William H. Mulcaster and manned by detachments of the Royal Newfoundland Regiment, harassed the troop transports and engaged them in a skirmish at French Creek about four miles downriver on November 3rd. The British gunboats caused the Americans enough damage and delay that they had time to return to Kingston and relate that Wilkinson's real target was Montreal.[2]

The British commander at Kingston had very few men to do anything about the planned attack. He had only two weak battallions of regulars, some of them just returned, battle weary, from the Detroit frontier. He gave Colonel J.W. Morrison 560 picked regulars from the garrison, which included elements of the Royal Newfoundland Regiment, and ordered him to pursue the Americans down the river in Captain Mulcaster's boats.

Morrison and Mulcaster eluded Chauncey's ships at the mouth of the St. Lawrence and gave swift pursuit to Wilkinson's army. By November 8th, they reached Prescott where they were reinforced by 270 militia and Indians. Morrison now had a force of 830 and he pressed on to the rapids of the St. Lawrence where Wilkinson was trying to quickly move down. Just above the rapids, the American commander had left Brigadier John Boyd and 1800 men to guard against attack by Morrison while he descended the rapids.

On the morning of November 11th, Morrison and Mulcaster's gunboats caught up to Wilkinson's rear guard at a place called Chrysler's Farm. The Americans were encamped in an open area and had spent a miserable night in snow and sleet when Mulcaster's gunboats surprised them

The "Battle of Chrysler's Farm" — on November 11, 1813 — saw a force of 800 British troops, Canadian militia, and Indians defeat a force of 1800 American infantry and cavalry.

and opened fire, scattering and disorganizing Boyd's troops. The Newfoundlanders in the gunboats directed their fire well and so pounded the Americans that Morrison had time to land his troops and form them into advancing files of attack.

Boyd rallied his men for a charge but the British repelled it quickly. He then ordered an attack to Morrison's left but the British Colonel quickly swung his files and once again beat back the Americans. In desperation, Boyd tried a third charge to Morrison's right but the British lines again quickly closed and drove the Americans back. All the while the British gunboats and their gunnery crews of the Newfoundland Regiment were blasting the disorganized American ranks, who by now were retreating from the field. As one observer recorded; "The 89th charged across the gully, re-formed and advanced with levelled bayonets. The foe retreated slowly at first, then broke and crowded down to where their boats lay."[3]

Of Boyd's 1800 men, he lost 439 to the casualty list: 102

men killed, 237 wounded, and 100 taken prisoner. Morrison's casualties by comparison were light; twenty-two men killed, 147 wounded, and twelve missing in action.[4] Of Morrison's twenty-two killed, one was an officer of the Royal Newfoundland Regiment, Captain Thomas Nairne, who had been detached as a field commander to the 49th Regiment. Two other officers of the Regiment, Captain John G. Heirliegh and Lieutenant Andrew H. Bulger, who were commanding their gunboats under Captain Mulcaster, were decorated for their leadership and bravery shown in the action at Chrysler's Farm.[5]

With the defeat of Boyd's force, Wilkinson was forced to retreat to the American side of the St. Lawrence and by the time he had regrouped his forces the time for an attack on Montreal was past. Winter had set in and so the Americans' grand scheme to capture Montreal had to be abandoned as the year of 1813 came to a close.

As the winter of 1813-1814 settled in upon the Canadian frontier bringing with it a bitterly cold, snow shrouded "forced" peace, the Royal Newfoundland Regiment was gathered at its headquarters in Kingston to take stock of its strength and condition. Sir George Prevost was of the opinion that the Regiment had been so decimated by casualties that it should be returned to Newfoundland to recruit replacements.

Of the original number of 683 which had been transferred from Newfoundland to Quebec in 1807, the Regiment had suffered 210 casualties from the outbreak of the war in June 1812 to the end of 1813. They had lost seventy-three killed in action, eighty-eight wounded, and fifty captured and interned as prisoners of war, or missing in action.[6]

At the beginning of 1814, the 473 men fit for service in the Regiment, a full 450 of them had been detached to Commander Yeo's Royal Navy "fleet" on Lake Ontario to serve as seamen and marines.[7] Prevost's recommendation to have the Regiment returned to Newfoundland to recruit replacements was taken under consideration by the high command in the War Office in London but was not acted upon until the summer of 1814. On June 21st, the War Office issued a General Order that "...directed that the Headquarters detachment of the Royal Newfoundland Fencibles would be held in readiness to embark for Newfoundland on one of the transports which was bringing the Nova Scotians to Quebec."[8]

But before this order was received by Governor Prevost, he had found another "special" duty for the versatile and accomplished Regiment. Following their capture of the Detroit frontier, the Americans cast their eyes towards Lake Michigan and their lost post on Michilimackinac Island. Their first loss of the war, it had remained unmolested in British hands since its capture. The Americans decided it was time to take it back.

Governor Prevost ordered Lieutenant Colonel Robert McDouall of the 8th Regiment of Foot to take two of the fittest companies of the Royal Newfoundland Regiment to Fort Mackinac to reinforce its garrison and replace the ailing and aging commander of the fort Capt. Charles Roberts. McDouall knew he would need men who were as at home on the water as they were on the land, and who knew how to build, repair and handle boats. He picked his Newfoundlanders from among those that had been serving as marines and seamen in Yeo's naval fleet, and departed York early in 1814 for the Nottawasaga River northwest of the Upper Canadian capital.

The route to Fort Mackinac was a long one and McDouall realized the need for a supply depot half-way between it and

York, its only supply base. During the winter, he had his Newfoundland "boatbuilders" construct thirty sturdy river-boats, as well as a blockhouse and outbuildings to house the supply depot of Nottawasaga.[9]

By April the boats were ready and McDouall and the Newfoundlanders sailed down the Nottawasaga River into Lake Huron. The lake was still clogged with breaking ice and the expedition took nearly a month to reach their destination. The true mettle of the Newfoundlanders was tried as they struggled their way in gale-force winds in the open boats among the thick ice-floes. They lost one of their boats, crushed by the ice, but otherwise arrived undamaged at Fort Mackinac on May 18th. Capt. Roberts was pleased to see his relief and expressed his "fullest confidence in the little de-tachment of the Royal Newfoundland Regiment."[10]

At Mackinac, McDouall learned that the Americans had recently completed a new post named Fort Gratoit at the head of the Detroit River on the foot of Lake Huron. They had also taken and occupied the British outpost at Prarie due Chien in the Indian country which the British felt they had to control if they were to keep the loyalty of the Indians and keep the Americans from expanding into the northwestern fur country. He decided to first take back Prarie du Chien, although he risked weakening his position at Mackinac, because he knew he would need the help of the Indians if the fort was attacked by the Americans from Fort Gratoit. He sent Major William McKay of the 5th Militia Corps of Lower Canada with a party of 200 Michigan Fencibles and Indians to do the task, while he prepared and reinforced his position at Fort Mackinac for the attack he knew would come.

On July 3rd, Ltd. Col. George Croghan, who had success-fully defended Fort Stephenson against Gen. Procter the summer before, left Detroit with five ships and a force of 700 men, regulars and Ohio militia to take Fort Mackinac. Croghan and his ships first sailed to St. Joseph's Island, intending to capture the British fort there, unaware that the British had abandoned the site once they had captured Fort Mackinac. The Americans' wasted time allowed McDouall to prepare his reception for them once they reached Fort Mackinac.

He had his company build breastworks at the only landing site on the island that was practical. The British themselves had used it two years before to surprise and capture the fort. McDouall did not intend to be surprised and when Croghan arrived on July 26th, the British commander was ready. He hurried his Newfoundlanders and Indians out of the fort and dispersed them at the landing site; the soldiers to the breastworks and the Indians into the surrounding woods from which they could fight in their most effective style. The fort itself—because of its high altitude was safe from the ships' cannon—and was left under the protection of 25 men of a local militia.

As expected, Croghan landed at McDouall's defensive site and was met by his Newfoundlanders, firing from behind their crude abatis of roots and branches and piled earth. The British cannon battered his force from the heights of the fort and he was forced to retreat into the woods. From there he attempted to flank the Newfoundlanders but he ran into McDouall's Indian force of 350 who were quite at home in this element.

The Indians sniped and disappeared, then reappeared to snipe again. In the thick woods, the Americans could not mount any concerted attack. Just as it seemed that the Americans were being held, McDouall received a report that more of the enemy were landing behind his position, between his force and the fort. He quickly withdrew his men to a position nearer the fort only to learn that the report he had received was false.[11]

Urgently, he rushed his lines back to their forward position, just in time to meet the Americans emerging from the woods. His Newfoundland regulars managed to hold the American advances long enough for the Indians to regroup in the woods and attack Croghan's flanks with chilling war cries and a hail of musket fire.

Unable to advance and under fire from his flanks, Croghan could only retreat to his landing site in the hope of escaping. His charge, even though he outnumbered the British two to one, was a foolhardy one since he had no advantage of surprise. His casualty list proved just how foolhardy. He lost twenty-two men killed and forty-four wounded. McDouall, almost miraculously, had lost only one of the Indians, killed.

After re-embarking his ships, Croghan sailed eastward, leaving two of his vessels, the *Scorpion* and the *Tigress* to run a blockade of Michilimackinac Island and cut off McDouall's supply of provisions from Nottawasaga in Georgian Bay. At the Nottawasaga depot, Lieutenant Miller Worsley of the Royal Navy was readying a cargo of supplies for McDouall and his men at Fort Mackinac when he heard there was an American fleet prowling Lake Huron. His being the only British ship on the lake and therefore the only transport for supplies to Mackinac, Worsley did not want to chance losing his vessel to the Americans.

With great labour, he and his crew dragged his tiny ship the *Nancy* up the shallow and winding Nottawasage River and attempted to hide it in a shallow cove with a camouflage of brush. Worsley then loaded the provisions for Fort Mackinac aboard a large Indian canoe and with the help of dark nights and not a little luck made the 350 mile passage along the north shore of Lake Huron to Michilimackinac Island.

His arrival there on August 31st, was just in time for the blockaded McDouall. The fort commandant had been reduced to rationing provisions for his soldiers and to killing horses to salt their meat to feed the Indians. He knew, however, that his plight had been only temporarily relieved. He had to break the blockade.[12]

Lt. Worsley, who had silently passed the two American ships in his canoe suggested that the ships could be taken by surprise in the same way he had succeeded in slipping past them. Desperate, McDouall agreed to Worsley's plan. On September 1st, he gave the lieutenant permission to man four boats and attempt to capture the two American ships. Worsley and his handful of Royal Navy seamen would man one of the boats, while the others would be manned by the marines of the Royal Newfoundland Regiment under the command of Lieutenant Andrew Bulger and two junior lieutenants of the regiment, Lieutenants Alfred Armstrong and John Radenhurst. That day, Worsley and his sailors, and Bulger and his marines, accompanied by two hundred Indians in their canoes left Mackinac in search of the American ships.

Near sunset on the next day, the British boats discovered one of the American vessels near a small group of islands and quietly concealed themselves while they planned their strike. About six o'clock the next evening they began rowing towards the ship which was about six miles away with "the most perfect order and silence."

About nine o'clock that evening as dusk was closing in Bulger's and Worsley's boats closed to within a hundred yards of the ship which they now identified as the *Tigress*, before they were spotted and hailed by a sentry. The British boats did not reply to the hailing and were within 30 feet of the ship before the sentry called an alarm.

As the crew scrambled on deck Bulger's marines and Worsley's sailors scooted up grappling ropes. Some of the American crew managed to get off some musket fire and others tried to bring the ship's guns into play. But by now it was too late. The Newfoundlanders and sailors gained the deck, quickly overpowering the ship's crew. Two of the sailors were killed and several of Bulger's marines wounded, but the prize was in hand.

Worsley sent the captured American crew back to Fort Mackinac in his boats and sent a canoe with scouts to locate the *Scorpion*. The scouts returned in a couple of hours to report that the American ship was headed towards them and about fifteen miles away. Unknowingly, but rightly, Worsley concluded that the *Tigress* was to rendezvous with the *Scorpion* and decided not to move the *Tigress*.

Late the next day, September 5th, the *Scorpion* approached the *Tigress* and anchored about two miles away. Lt. Bulger described what followed:

> The position of the *Tigress* was not altered, and the better to carry on the deception the American Pendant was kept flying. On the 5th Inst we discovered the Enemy's schooner beating up to us, the Soldiers I directed to keep below, or to lie down on the Deck to avoid being seen. Everything succeeded to our wish, the enemy came to anchor about two miles from us in the night, and as the day dawned on the 6th Inst we slipt (sic. slipped) our cable and ran down under our Jib and Foresail. Everything was so well managed by Lt. Worsley that we were within ten yards of the enemy before they discovered us. It was then too late, for in the course of five minutes her deck was covered with our men and the British flag hoisted over the American.[13]

The American schooners *Tigress* and *Scorpion* after their capture by Lt. Bulgar and the "marines" of
the Royal Newfoundland Regiment, were sailed to the British stronghold at Fort Mackinac.

The British now had their second prize, but it did not
come without a cost. One sailor was killed and eight of the
Newfoundland marines wounded, including Lt. Bulger himself who suffered a "severe chest wound." McDouall had
secured his supply route and in the process had acquired
himself a "fleet" for Lake Huron thanks to the courage and
tenacity of the Royal Newfoundland Regiment. As Bulger
modestly put it to his commander McDouall, "...I must

assure you that every Officer and Man did his Duty."
McDouall needed no assurance. He wrote his superiors in
Kingston that Lt. Bulger and his brother officers, who "with
the detachment of the brave Newfoundland Regiment (who
are familiar with this kind of service) merit my entire approbation."[14]

McDouall's troubles however were not over. While he
waited for the American attack on Fort Mackinac the Americans had once again attempted to capture Fort McKay at
Prarie du Chien. He decided that the outpost needed a
regular army officer to take charge of it and he chose Lt.
Bulger as the man for the job. Although not yet fully recovered from his wound, Bulger unquestioningly accepted the
duty. McDouall allowed Bulger to take a company of the
Royal Newfoundland Regiment with him but he did not
order which ones were to go. Bulger asked for volunteers and
immediately found himself having to pick fifty men from
among the nearly 100 of the Regiment still fit for duty.

Bulger's Newfoundlanders were quickly dubbed the
"Mississippi Volunteers" and by the end of October they
were ready for the long, gruelling 500 mile voyage from
Mackinac to the isolated wilderness of Prarie due Chien at
the junction of the Wisconsin and Mississippi Rivers. The
trek took Bulger and his "Volunteers" a month to complete
the brutal trip. He reported to McDouall on December 30th
the details of his journey.

"I reached this place on the 30th November," he wrote his
commander, "From the moment of my departure from Green
Bay...until my arrival here I experienced every misery in the
power of cold and want to inflict.

"I suffered more, Sir, during this voyage than you can at
all imagine — much more than ever I have suffered during
the whole course of my life before."[15]

Bulger and his "Mississippi Volunteers" found Fort McKay to be in near chaos. The posts' buildings were in various states of disrepair or had not been completed at all. The militia companies which manned the fort were unruly and undisciplined and the numerous Indians there grumbled and complained about the lack of food and provisions they had come to expect from their British benefactors.

Captain Bulger (for he had been given a field commission to that rank upon taking up the duty at Prarie du Chien) soon had the situation in hand, and backed up by his disciplined and loyal "Volunteers" of the Royal Newfoundland Regiment had formulated a plan by the spring of 1815 to carry the war to the Americans down the Mississippi River to St. Louis rather than wait for the Americans to bring it to them.

He was ready to begin his assault in May, when on the 15th of that month he received word from the east that the War of 1812 had been ended by the signing of the Treaty of Ghent on Christmas Eve, 1814, four and one half months ago. Capt. Bulger and his "Mississippi Volunteers" were recalled to Lake Huron where they awaited further orders.[16]

PROFILE: TREATY OF GHENT

The war of 1812-1814 was not even a year old when both countries involved began to look for a way to stop it. The British not only did not want the war, but also did not need it. They had their hands full with Napoleon in Europe. The Americans did not want the war either, but they did want territorial and economic concessions from Britain. By going to war they showed the English that they meant business and hoped that their bluff would force the English to negotiate with them.

As early as March of 1813, the contestants were looking for a way out. An unlikely mediator entered the dispute in the person of Tsar Alexander I of Russia who offered to mediate the dispute. The Tsar proposed solutions but the British were not willing to negotiate through a third party. But the Tsar's idle meddling soon desisted as he found Napoleon on his doorstep and himself in great need of the British as an ally.[17]

The war dragged on another year when once again Britain and the United States approached each other in an attempt to end the conflict. In August both sides agreed to send negotiators to Belgium to try to hammer out a conclusion acceptable to both sides. After haggling over just where in Belgium the talks should be held, the city of Ghent was decided on, it having a long history of neutrality.

The talks took almost five months, most of the protracted time probably owing to the Americans who sent a delegation almost twice as large as the British, and to a great extent, divided among itself. Among the five American negotiators were hawks, doves, and moderates. One of them, John Quincy Adams, who was later to become President of the United States, found himself often at odds with another,

Henry Clay, who was one of the "War Hawks" who had been in favour of invading Canada.[18]

The British, who regarded the negotiations at Ghent as secondary to those of Vienna where more important ones were taking place concerning the peace in Europe, sent a less experienced and capable delegation than the Americans. It was headed by Lord Gambier, a former Royal Navy Admiral who had little experience in diplomacy, and assisted by Henry Goulburn, a British M.P. and under-secretary of state for war, and Dr. William Adams who was considered an expert in Maritime law.

After weeks of bickering — among delegates between themselves as well as with the opposing side — an agenda was finally agreed upon. Three issues were to be discussed, although a fourth one which both sides thought of great importance — the fishery off the coasts of Newfoundland and Labrador — was kept out of the discussions by mutual consent of both sides. For discussion were the issues of British impressment of American seamen on the high seas, the establishment of an Indian "state" in the northwest, and a re-negotiation of the boundaries between the United States and the "provinces" of Canada agreed upon in 1783.

All the issues were in the better interests of the United States and the British saw no reason to make any concessions regarding any of them. The "Indian Territory" in the northwest between the Ohio Valley and the Mississippi River they had won from the French by their victory on the Plains of Abraham. The impressment of American sailors on the high seas would end as soon as the business with Napoleon was concluded, and as for the boundaries of the U.S. and Canada, the Americans had been given all they were going to get in the treaty of 1783.

The negotiation dragged on for weeks, then months, as

each side hopefully waited for news from America that would tell them of some victory or turnaround in the war that would give them an upper hand in the negotiations. The British dragged their heels and ran a bluff. The Americans complained that, "The British plenipotentiaries have invariably referred to their Government every note received from us, and waited for the return of their message before they have transmitted to us their answer."[19]

The Americans waited out the British bluff and it worked. The British were the first to move, and it was on the question of an Indian state. They were willing to give up their alliance with the Indian tribes of the northwest provided that the Americans also agreed not to employ them as allies in wartime. Outwardly, the Americans protested this as a concession, but secretly regarded it as a gain. Such an arrangement would allow them to move into an unaligned Indian "state" and woo the natives into their camp, just as the British had done following the American Revolution.

As the year 1814 drew to a close, the Americans saw their hopes of winning by diplomacy what they were failing to do by warfare, also dimming. France was beaten, and Russia, to which they had also made overtures for help, had shifted its alliances and isolated itself from the other major European powers. Too, news from the homefront was not good. After one and one half years of a war that had been started by the United States to gain more territory, they now held less than they had when the war begun.

The British held half of the territory of Maine, the Niagara frontier, Fort Mackinac and their posts on the upper lakes and in Prairie du Chien country, as well as territory at the head of Lake Superior. The Americans held only the British forts at Amherstburg and Erie. It was proposed to the Americans that as far as boundaries went, the British were willing

to return to the "status quo" as it had been before the outbreak of the war. The Americans decided to grab their bless-
ings and give silent thanks. As for settling the real issues over
which the war had started, nothing was resolved. The question of impressment on the high seas, the real issue of Indian
land rights, and the American claim to fishing rights on the
Atlantic coast, were all hidden away with an agreement that
they would be discussed at a later time. All agreed to call
what was really a truce by another name — the Peace Treaty
of Ghent.

On Christmas Eve, 1814, the eight peace negotiators of
England and the United States sat down to read and sign the
terms of the treaty that saw "both sides agree to disagree on
everything except the conclusion of hostilities." The next
day, the peace negotiators sat down to a Christmas dinner of
prime beef and plum pudding brought across the English
Channel especially for them. A band played "God Save the
King" and "Yankee Doodle" and toasts were offered to King
George III and President James Madison. "Outside, the
church bells of Ghent were ringing in honour of the birthday
of the Prince of Peace."[20]

The great pomp, ceremony and civility that attended the
signing of the "Peace of Ghent" in Europe did not reach the
snow shrouded forests and farmlands of Canada and America until months later. In the meantime, men continued to
fight and die in a war that nobody wanted, and once it had
begun, nobody seemed to know how to stop. Before word of
the treaty reached all of the farflung outposts of both the
Americans and the British in North America, almost 18,000
men had become casualties in the War of 1812-1814. These
were the casualties that could be counted. Thousands more
among the farmsteads and isolated villages of the frontier, as

well as among the Indian tribes who kept no tallies, can also be counted among them.[21]

John Quincy Adams, later President of the United States and one of the negotiators of the "Peace at Ghent," later wrote, "True it is that the peace of Ghent was in its nature and character a truce, rather than a peace. Neither party gave up anything: all the points of collision between them which have subsisted before the war were left open...nothing was set-tled—nothing in substance but an indefinite suspension of hostilities was agreed to."[22]

Endnotes:

1. Raddall; op. cit., p. 260-261.
2. Berton; op. cit., p. 230.
3. Saunders; op. cit., p. 39.
4. Stanley; op. cit., p. 265.
5. Saunders; op. cit., p. 9. Captain Thomas Nairne, from all accounts was a very popular officer among the British forces in Quebec. As Saunders writes: "He was so much thought of that the authorities in Quebec got permission from those responsible for burying the men and officers on Chrysler's Field and they sent a man down with a sleigh, took up Captain Nairne and dragged him on the sleigh all the way over the snow to Quebec. The funeral, it is said, was one of the largest attended ever held in the historic fortress of Quebec."
6. Nicholson; op. cit., p. 81.
7. Saunders; op. cit., p. 37.
8. Nicholson; op. cit., p. 81.
9. Stanley; op. cit., p. 239.
10. Nicholson; op. cit., p. 288.
11. Berton; op. cit., p. 311.
12. Stanley; op. cit., p. 294.
13. Nicholson; op. cit., p. 83.
14. Ibid.
15. Saunders; op. cit., p. 21.
16. Nicholson; op. cit., p. 84.
17. Stanley; op. cit., p. 382.
18. Raddall; op. cit., p. 321.
19. Saunders, Dr. Robert; "The Peace of Ghent and the End of the War of 1812." *Newfoundland Quarterly*, p. 29.
20. Stanley; op. cit., p. 393.
21. Raddall; op. cit., p. 324.
22. Saunders; op. cit., p.33.

EPILOGUE

"Forgotten" Warriors

HE TREATY OF GHENT and the end of the War of 1812-14, cast the tiny remnant of the Royal Newfoundland Regiment still in the Canadas into a sort of surreal limbo. Captain Bulger and his "Mississippi Volunteers" along with the small company at Fort Mackinac were withdrawn to Manitoulin Island in Lake Huron where they sat idle as they watched the Americans take repossession of Michilimackinac Island and the fort they had fought so gallantly to defend.

Later that summer they were withdrawn to Quebec City where they joined a small remnant of the Regiment which had not been sent back to their homeland the previous summer. In September of 1815, the remnant of the Regiment was embarked for St. John's, returning to their homes which they had not seen in ten years. Among them were the prisoners of war, some of whom had languished in the miserable prisons of Kentucky and Ohio for over a year; most of whom were so ill "that not one in twenty who were called well would ever recover their strength and appearance."[1]

Back home, the Regiment was given the duty of garrisoning the town of St. John's. Its full complement now numbered only twenty-three officers and 315 men of other ranks. Attempts were made to recruit men to fill its complement, but

Newfoundland Military Museum (Photo: B.D. Fardy)

Prisoners of War: In the War of 1812, women and children who were the families of soldiers captured after battle, were also held with their husbands. These first prisoner of war camps were miserable hovels, which lacked everything from proper food to medical attention. Most of those who survived them, left them in broken health and never fully recovered.

the all too alive memories of the nearly one-half of the men who went away to the Canadas and did not return, kept most from wanting to follow in their ghostly path.

The Royal Newfoundland Regiment served in its peaceful capacity at St. John's for a year and a half. During that time Major Heathcote and his scarred veterans, bloodied on the field of battle, found themselves in a new "war"— the paper chase war. Heathcote found himself pestered with administrative duties, answering demands for explanations of expenditures on everything from bed sheets to sheet iron which had been billed against the Regiment on a war-trail that took them from St. John's to the Mississippi River. Obviously, the paper shufflers of bureaucracy in London did not understand what the wages of war were.[2]

In May of 1816 the Prince Regent ordered that all Fencible Corps in North America were to be reduced. The Royal Newfoundland Regiment was one of those Regiments designated to be disbanded. With the demise of the Regiment it also seemed that the memory of their selfless actions of gallantry and dedication also faded from the minds of the people they had patriotically rallied to defend in a war that nobody really wanted.

The deeds and memories of the hundreds of men who had rallied so valiantly from the tiny isolated population of Newfoundland languished and dimmed for 100 years after the end of the War of 1812-1814. Then, almost 100 years after the heroic Regiment of 1812 had been disbanded in 1816, Britain once again called on its small island colony for strong hearts and stout backs to defend freedom from tyranny.

In 1914, sons of the sons of the gallant Royal Newfoundland Regiment resurrected the proud tradition of their forefathers and once again marched off to foreign shores, to defend and serve King and country, all of whom were to offer — and many of whom would pay — the supreme sacrifice.

Endnotes:

1. Nicholson; op. cit., p. 84. As Nicholson writes: "They were without blankets; few had tents; rations issued irregularly, were often not fit to eat; and there was little or no medical attention for the many who were sick. Half starved and already weakened by months of privations as prisoners of war, they fell easy victims to fever."

2. Ibid., p. 84.

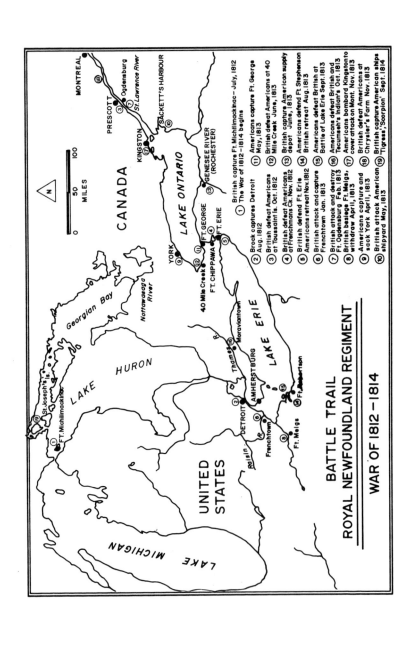

BATTLE TRAIL
ROYAL NEWFOUNDLAND REGIMENT

WAR OF 1812–1814

① British capture Ft. Michilimackinac— July, 1812
① The War of 1812–1814 begins
② Brock captures Detroit Aug. 1812
③ British defeat Americans at Toussaint Is. Oct. 1812
④ British defeat Americans at Frenchmans Ck. Nov. 1812
⑤ British defend Ft. Erie Americans retreat Nov. 1812
⑥ British attack and capture Frenchtown Jan. 1813
⑦ British attack and destroy Ft. Ogdensburg Feb. 1813
⑧ British besiege Ft. Meigs, withdraw April, 1813
⑨ Americans capture and sack York April, 1813
⑩ British attack American shipyard May, 1813
⑪ Americans capture Ft. George May, 1813
⑫ British defeat Americans at 40 Mile Creek June, 1813
⑬ British capture American supply depot June, 1813
⑭ Americans defend Ft. Stephenson British retreat Aug. 1813
⑮ Americans defeat British at Battle of Lake Erie Sept. 1813
⑯ Americans defeat British and Tecumseh's Indian's Oct. 1813
⑰ Americans bombard Kingston to cover attack on Mont. Nov. 1813
⑱ British defeat Americans at Chrysler's Farm Nov. 1813
⑲ British capture American ships Tigress, Scorpion Sept. 1814

Bibliography

Allen, Robert S. "Sir Isaac Brock." *Canadian Encyclopedia, Vol. I.* Hurtig Pub. Co. Edmonton, Alta. 1988.

Arnett, Tom. "The Battle of Lundy's Lane." *Canadian Frontier.* Nunaga Pub. Co., Surrey, B.C. 1976.

Berton, Pierre. *Flames Across the Border.* McClelland & Stewart, Toronto, Ont. 1981.

Berton, Pierre. *The Invasion of Canada.* McClelland & Stewart, Toronto, Ont. 1980.

Berton, Pierre. "The War of 1812." *Canadian Encyclopedia, Vol. 4.* Hurtig Pub. Co., Edmonton, Alta. 1988.

Bronson, L.N. "The Search for Tecumseh." *Canadian Frontier.* Garnet Pub. Co. Ltd., Vancouver, B.C. 1974

Calvert, Michael, and Peter Young. *A Dictionary of Battles: 1715-1815.* Mayflower Books, New York, N.Y. 1979.

Candow, James E. "The British Army in Newfoundland." *Newfoundland Quarterly.* Vol. 14, No. 2, St. John's, Nfld. 1983.

Careless, J.M.S., *Colonists and Canadians: 1760-1867.* McMillan and Co., Ltd., Toronto. 1971.

Christie, Carl A. "The Battle of Beaver Dams." *Canadian Frontier.* Antonson Publishing Ltd. Surrey, B.C. 1977.

Cochrane, Hugh F. "The Battle of York." *Canadian Frontier.* Garnet Pub. Co. Ltd., Vancouver, B.C. 1973.

Cochrane, Hugh F. "Tiger in the Forest." *Canadian Frontier.* Nunaga Pub. Co. Ltd., Surrey, B.C. 1976.

Dowd, Gregory Evans. *A Spirited Resistance.* Johns Hopkins University Press. Baltimore and London. 1992.

Dupuy, Ernest and Trevor N. Dupuy. *An Outline History of the American Revolution.* Harper & Row. New York. 1975.

Dyer, Gwynne and Tina Viljoen. *The Defence of Canada.* McClelland & Stewart Inc. Toronto. 1990.

Every, Dale Van. *A Company of Heroes.* William Morrow Co. Ltd. New York, N.Y. 1962.

Every, Dale Van. *The Final Challenge.* William Morrow Co. Ltd. New York, N.Y. 1964.

Fardy, B.D. "Signal Hill: Last Battle for Canada." *Great Stories from the Canadian Frontier.* Antonson Publishing Inc. Surrey, B.C. 1979.

Fardy, B.D. *Under Two Flags.* Creative Publishers, St. John's, Nfld. 1987.

Hannon, Leslie F. *Canada At War.* McClelland & Stewart, Toronto, Ont. 1968.

Harrington, Michael F. "Offbeat History." *The Evening Telegram.* St. John's, Nfld. Feb, 21, 1977; Jan. 16, 1978; Jan. 11, 1982; July 5, 1982; Jan. 10, 1983; Sept. 17, 1984; Nov. 10, 1986; July 4, 1988; Nov. 7, 1988; Jan. 9, 1989; Dec. 31, 1990; Nov. 4, 1991; Nov. 11, 1991.

Hill, Douglas. *The Opening of the Canadian West.* William Heinmann Ltd. London-Toronto. 1967.

Hook, Jason. *American Indian Warrior Chief.* Firebird Books, Dorset, England. 1989.

Ketchum, Richard M., editor. *The American Revolution.* American Heritage Pub. Co., New York, N.Y. 1971.

Lanctot, Dr. Gustave. "When Newfoundland Saved Canada." *Newfoundland Quarterly.* Vol. 49, No. 3, 1949.

Lanctot, Dr. Gustave. "When Newfoundland Helped Save Canada." *Book of Newfoundland.* Vol. 6, St. John's Book Publishers (1967) Ltd. St. John's, Nfld. 1975.

Martin, Ged. "Newfoundland at the Time of the French Attack of 1796." *Newfoundland Quarterly.* Vol. 6, No 4, St. John's, Nfld. 1974.

McKenzie, Ruth. *Laura Secord: The Legend and the Lady.* McClelland & Stewart, Toronto, Ont. 1971.

Mearling, S.R. "Guy Carleton: 1st Baron of Dorchester." *Canadian Encyclopedia Vol. I.* Hurtig Publishers. Edmonton, Alta. 1988.

Morris, Don. "In History: Eight Soldiers Meet Fate on Gallows After Aborted Mutiny." *The Express.* St. John's, Nfld. Feb. 19, 1992.

Morris, Don. "In History: Mutiny on the Waterfront." *The Express.* St. John's, Nfld. June 30, 1991.

Mustard, Cam and Amy Zierler. *Signal Hill: An Illustrated History.* Nfld. Historical Trust Co-op. St. John's, Nfld. 1982.

Nicholson, Col. G.W.L. *The Fighting Newfoundlander.* Government of Newfoundland and Labrador, St. John's, Nfld. 1964.

O'Flaherty, Maj. John F. "The Royal Newfoundland Regiment." *Book of Newfoundland.* Vol. 4. Nfld. Book Publishers (1967) Ltd. St. John's, Nfld. 1967.

O'Neill, Paul. *A Seaport Legacy.* Press Porcepic. Erin, Ont. 1975.

O'Neill, Paul. *The Oldest City.* Press Porcepic. Erin, Ont. 1975.

Parkman, Francis. *Montcalm and Wolfe.* Penguin Books Canada, Ltd. Toronto, Ont. 1984.

Prowse, D.W. *A History of Newfoundland: From the Colonial Records.* McMillan and Co. Ltd. London, New York. 1895.

Raddall, Thomas H. *The Path of Destiny.* Doubleday Canada Ltd. Toronto, Ont. 1957.

Rawlyk, G.A. *Revolution Rejected: 1775-1776.* Prentice-Hall Canada. Scarborough, Ont. 1968.

Rowe, Frederick W. *A History of Newfoundland and Labrador*. McGrath-Hill Ryerson. Toronto, Montreal. 1980.

Saunders, Dr. Robert. "A Forgotten Hero (Admiral Saunders)." *Newfoundland Quarterly*. Vol. 62, No. 1, St. John's, Nfld. 1963.

Saunders, Dr. Robert. "A Forgotten Hero (Admiral Saunders) II." *Newfoundland Quarterly*. Vol. 62, No. 2, St. John's, Nfld. 1963.

Saunders, Dr. Robert. "The Peace of Ghent and the War of 1812." *Newfoundland Quarterly*. Vol. 60, No. 4, St. John's, Nfld. 1961.

Saunders, Dr. Robert. "The Royal Newfoundland Regiment and the Royal Scots." *Newfoundland Quarterly*. Vol. 60, No. 1, St. John's, Nfld. 1961.

Saunders, Dr. Robert. "When Newfoundland Helped Save Canada." *Newfoundland Quarterly*. St. John's, Nfld. (Vols. & Nos.) 50-3:1950; 50-4:1951; 51-1:1951; 51-2:1951; 51-3:1951; 52-3:1951; 53-1:1954; 53-2:1954; 53-3:1954; 53-5:1954; 54-1:1955; 54-2:1955; 54-4:1955; 55-3:1956; 56-1:1957; 56-2:1957; 56-3:1957; 56-4:1957; 57-1:1958; 57-2:1958; 57-3:1958; 57-4:1958; 58-1:1959; 58-3:1959; 59-1:1960; 59-4:1960; 60-2:1961; 61-1:1962; 61-3:1962; 62-3:1963; 64-1:1965.

Silvester, William. "Michilimackinac: The Bloodless War." *Canadian Frontier*. Nunaga Publishing Co. Ltd. Surrey, B.C. 1976.

Stanley, George F.G. *The War of 1812*. MacMillan of Canada — Nat'l Museums of Canada, Ottawa, Ont. 1983.

Steele, Betty. "Newfoundlanders Who Saved Canada." *Atlantic Advocate*. Halifax, N.S. March — 1981.

Tanner, Odgen, *The Canadians*. Time-Life Books, Alexandria, Virginia. 1977.

Webber, David. "The Military History of St. John's." *Book of Newfoundland*. Vol. 6. St. John's Book Publishers (1967) Ltd. St. John's, Nfld. 1975.

Webber, David. "The Recapture of St. John's: 1762." *Occasional Paper Vol. 1, No. 1*. Newfoundland Naval and Military Museum. St. John's, Nfld. 1962.

Whalen, Dwight. "Laura Secord: Heroine of Upper Canada." *Canadian Frontier*. Garnet Pub. Co. Ltd. Vancouver, B.C. 1973.

Whalen, Dwight. "The Restless Tombs of Isaac Brock." *Canadian Frontier*. Garnet Pub. Co. Ltd. Vancouver, B.C. 1974.

White, Jack A. "Streets of St. John's: Fort Townshend." *The Evening Telegram*. St. John's, Nfld. April 23, 1988.